lots og

Hardcore from the Heart

h that

a sweet

of a.

boyfriend. Nice!

love

Annie Sprinkle

Critical Performances

Series editors: Lynda Hart and Paul Heritage

Combining performative texts with critical theory and personal reflection, each volume in the series pairs a performance artist/playwright with a critical theorist in a dialogue aimed to elucidate both disciplines. These books are designed both as critical introductions to the artists and as scholarly introductions to the field at large.

Published books in the series:

Of All the Nerve: Deb Margolin SOLO, edited by Lynda Hart

Rachel's Brain and Other Storms: The Performance Scripts of Rachel Rosenthal, edited by Una Chaudhuri

Hardcore from the Heart

The Pleasures, Profits and Politics of Sex in Performance

Annie Sprinkle: SOLO

Edited and with Commentaries by Gabrielle Cody

CONTINUUM
London and New York

Continuum
The Tower Building, 11 York Road, London SE1 7NX
370 Lexington Avenue, New York, NY 10017-6503

First published 2001

British Library Cataloguing-in-Publication Data
A catalogue record for this book is available from the British Library.

ISBN 0-8264-4892-5 (hardback)
    0-8264-4893-3 (paperback)

Library of Congress Cataloging-in-Publication Data
Sprinkle, Annie, 1954–
    Hardcore from the heart: the pleasures, profits and politics of sex in performance/Annie Sprinkle: SOLO; edited and with commentaries by Gabrielle Cody.
        p. cm. — (Critical performances)
    Includes bibliographical references.
    Filmography: p.
    ISBN 0-8264-4892-5 — ISBN 0-8264-4893-3 (pbk.)
    1. Sprinkle, Annie, 1954– I. Cody, Gabrielle, 1956– II. Title. III. Series.

PN2287.S6645 A25 2001
791.43′028′092—dc21

                                                    00-065695

Designed and typeset by Paston Prepress, Beccles, Suffolk
Printed and bound in Great Britain by Biddles Ltd, Guildford and King's Lynn

Contents

Foreword: Ooouuuhhh, Professor, I Love It When You
    Talk Academic *by Rebecca Schneider*   vii
Acknowledgments   xi

Introduction: Sacred Bazoombas *by Gabrielle Cody*   1

Part I: Actions, Rituals, Performances
    Strip Speak: Nurse Sprinkle's Sex Education Class   23
    Metamorphosexual MudBath Ritual: A Private
        Performance   27
    MetamorphoSex   31
    Peace in Bed   37
    Liberty Love Boat   41
    Annie Sprinkle's Herstory of Porn   45
    Commentary: *Annie Sprinkle from Reel to Real*   65

Part II: Pornographos: Writings of a Prostitute
    My Brushes and Crushes with the Law   73
    Dear Friends and Lovers at 848   78
    You've Come a Long Way Baby: Twelve Steps to Cure
        Sex Worker Burnout   80
    Commentary: *A Labor of Love*   82

Part III: Interviews: A Movable Feast
    Annie's Breakfast with Veronica Vera: The Art of Sex Work   87
    Lunch at the Art/Life Institute: A Conversation with
        Linda M. Montano, Barbara Carrellas, and Gabrielle Cody   93
    Dinner with Richard Schechner and Gabrielle Cody:
        She Wanted a Better Life   105
    Annie's Dessert with Mae Tyme, an Anti-Porn Feminist   111
    Gabrielle's Midnight Snack with Monika Treut   119

Outroduction   123

Selected Performances, Filmography and Bibliography   127

Foreword

Ooouuuhhh, Professor, I Love It When You Talk Academic

Rebecca Schneider

Contemporary feminist performance artists present their own bodies beside or relative to the history of reading the body marked female, the body rendered consumable and consumptive in representation. In this sense, the contemporary explicit body performer consciously and emphatically stands beside herself, in that she grapples overtly with the history of her body's explication, wrestling with the ghosts of that explication. Given this 'standing beside,' or 'sidestepping' to borrow from Elin Diamond (1989:68), feminist artists can be understood to present their bodies as dialectical images.

'Dialectical image' is a phrase used by Walter Benjamin to refer to an object or constellation of objects which tell the secret – which reveal or expose the traces of their false promises, their secret(ed) service to the dreamscapes of modernism. Dialectical images are objects which show the show, which make it apparent that they are not entirely that which they have been given to represent – the way cracks in face paint or runs in mascara might show the material in tension with the constructed ideal. Like secrets bared, dialectical images evidence commodity dreamscapes as bearing secrets, as propped up by masquerade. For Benjamin, prostitutes present prime dialectical images. As 'commodity and seller in one,' prostitutes show the show of their commodification and cannot completely pass as that which they purport to be. Dialectical images such as prostitutes (Benjamin also cites used or outmoded commodities, cracked or discarded promises) can talk or gesture back to the entire social enterprise which secret(e)s them. For Benjamin, reading dialectical images for the secrets they tell and the memories they hold provides a counter-history to modernity's myriad promises. Objects accumulating in the cracks of dreams, in the promises of 'Progress,' can be read back against pervasive myths of nature, value, and social order. Dialectical images are runes and can be recognized as the debris secreted (in both senses of that word) by the mandates of capitalist dreamscapes.

Dialectical images provoke a viewer/reader to think again – to take a second look. It is somehow in the flickering undecidability between the viewing subject's reading and the object's cracks (exposing masquerade) that dialectical images threaten to work. The challenge in engaging dialectical images seems to lie somewhere in between – a space at once exceedingly private, full of located and personal particulars of reading, and radically public, full of socially inscribed dreamscapes, pretexts for reading. The crack of this space between the personal particular and the socially inscribed is a fraught space. It is a space which feminist performance artists and cultural critical theorists writing on performativity have approached as deeply imbricated in the social dynamics of the marked body.

Into this fraught space I found myself repeatedly placing a specific contemporary performance artist, pornographer and prostitute, Annie Sprinkle, as one places a question mark. In my mind, Sprinkle also sat at the threshold of the 'both/and,' the messy impasse between essentialist and constructivist critiques of gender. Sprinkle's work became, for me, problematically emblematic of the tense stand-off between the literal, material body and her complex ghosting, the symbolic body of 'woman.'

The theater has a long tradition of the kind of humor that hits you in the gut with its not-at-all-funny flip side, just as you are laughing. In fact, sorrow or pity at the edges of laughter, and laughter in response to the horrific, is so prevalent that the ancient Western habit of segregating comedy and tragedy begins to seem, itself, ludicrous. The ancient Greek distinction is so bound up, however, with agendas of the State and regulation of emotional and libidinal energies of the polis, as well as with archivization (only tragedies were housed in the official archives), that we would be remiss not to recall what the distinction between tragedy and comedy has enabled, if not engendered, in terms of Western segregated ways of knowing. Still, if the tragic and the comic were religiously segregated in classical and then again in neoclassical traditions, popular festive forms (and modernist forms which emulated the popular) have long made a mess of those boundaries, often through the medium of parodic inversion or the grotesque.

As a performer who talks back to her socio-cultural hailing as 'whore,' a hailing she volubly insists is honorary, it should be no surprise that what comes out of Sprinkle's mouth and across in her actions as praise for her noble profession at first appears as ludic inversion. The ludic inversion, however, could not be more serious. If the name 'whore,' like the words 'queer' or 'nigger' or 'spic,' has been as effectively deployed as an injurious appellation, Sprinkle is engaged in flipping that injury back against the historical force of its deployment. By greeting the injurious hailing with a hearty 'Yes! It's me!' she strategically confounds the hailing, forcing it to ricochet against its investments and intentions.

In the course of writing *The Explicit Body in Performance* (1997) I was gainfully employed in a number of speaking engagements. One such engagement was a panel at New York University, to which I was invited to present some of the material below. Wonderfully, Annie Sprinkle was also on the panel, speaking about her artwork. I was, of course, nervous about the power dynamics, or at least the tense space, between theorist and practitioner: the sometimes unfortunate ways in which theorists are given to speak for the subject they hail without always positioning their own institutionally privileged and often disembodied 'authorities' as voices – voices driven by the very language systems that have interpellated their artist-subjects, specifically female artist-subjects, as delimited to the sexualized body. I tried to address this anxiety in the talk I presented, not entirely successfully in my own estimation. If Sprinkle's work was often read as 'funny,' I was concerned that my serious theoretical engagement with the forcefulness of that humor might realign it within a problematic victimizing reading for the tragic – just as Sprinkle was struggling to flip the injury against itself, to show up, that is, the ludicrous bases of the social Tragedy of prostitution.

In response to my anxiety Sprinkle was, as Sprinkle is, extremely generous. A short while after the talk she presented me with a large black-and-white poster of her 'Bosom Ballet' – a series of images of her breasts, held in her two gloved hands and manipulated in a series of pirouettes, pliés, and grands jetés. Across the bottom of the poster she had written in a lovely cursive with red lipstick the line 'Oooouuuhhh, Rebecca, I love it when you talk Academic.' This was followed by a big red lipstick kiss print. My anxiety – that my language would colonize her actions – was clearly my own problem. It made me laugh but it also drove home, for me, the fact that my own anxiety was riddled with the very assumptions I strove to resist. Sprinkle was literalizing the scene of seduction – here making quite explicit the seduction of theory-speak – and flipping back to me my own engagement in the seductions I naïvely (if institutionalized habits of blindness can be called naïve) misrecognized as of the 'other.' I was honored.

Some time later, as part of a job interview, I stood in a large auditorium and presented, again, some of the work from *The Explicit Body in Performance*. As was often the case at these talks, I used slides. This particular auditorium was 'state of the art,' so the slides were illuminated gigantically behind me on an absolutely huge screen. I felt like a midget at a podium, gesturing ludicrously at the slide of Sprinkle, legs akimbo, flashlight shining at her cervix. A moment of panic hit me when I looked over my shoulder and witnessed the gigantic proportions of the image. Words left me. I turned back to my audience and saw them seeing me having just seen Sprinkle – the size of her cervix alone bigger than my head.

There was a moment of uncomfortable silence – then everyone laughed. I'm still not sure what to think about the scene, except to accept the humor of the moment as, perhaps, akin to the force of Sprinkle's critique. Sure, some folks won't 'get' the barbed edges of the joke, as it appears to recapitulate the same violence that has delimited women to sexuality throughout patriarchy, but in point of fact, I was a female academic in the running for a prestigious job talking about Sprinkle's 'oooouvre' – taking it seriously and being taken seriously. We deserve, as Cixous and Clement suggested after Medusa, to laugh.

During the question and answer session I was asked the very question I'd fretted about so often. I was asked whether or not, as an academic, I was exploiting the prostitute – in some senses her fixed reproduction in an image behind me subjected her to my 'take' quite forcefully (though no one seems to trouble art historians for displaying Manet's *Olympia* and pontificating). I myself was an 'authority figure' speaking for the artist/prostitute, etc. etc. My response came quickly. I'm not exactly clear about what's at stake in our continuing to wield distinctions that bear troubling, I said. I'm especially concerned that we follow Sprinkle and trouble borders between artist (masculinized) and prostitute (feminized), or academic (masculinized) and prostitute (feminized). Perhaps we should consider Schneider as the prostitute and Sprinkle as the theorist? Who's to say I'm not for sale? This is a job interview, isn't it? I was offered the position, and I assumed it.

Acknowledgments

Annie Sprinkle would like to thank the following beautiful people who made this book possible: Gaby Cody for choosing me to do this book with and being a delightful collaborator. The Continuum folks for publishing it. Lynda Hart for inviting us to be in this series and coming up with the Critical Performances concept. Rebecca Schneider for her foreword. My Mom and Dad for taking me to the theater a lot as a kid. Hilary Sio, the angel on Gaby's shoulder. Kimberly Silver, Emilio Cubeiro, Scarlot Harlot, Daniel Banks, Willem de Ridder, Les Barany and Terry Horowitz for helping me 'put on a show.' The people at the Cowell, the Vortex, The Harmony Burlesque and the Schmidt Theaters for being brave and free enough to present my new theater work. Club 90. Joseph Kramer for being an awesome friend. Katherine Gates for expanding my communications networks. Alexa Torgerson, our patient intern for her assistance. Wendy Weckwerth for her help on the manuscript. Cathy O'Dell for teaching the History of Performance Art course that got me on the path. Linda Lovelace, Gypsy Rose Lee and Margo St James for showing me that sex work is about far more than sex. To my girlfriend Captain Barb Roddy for the delicious dyke-mermaid love. Dieter Jarzombec, Carol Queen, Robert Lawrence, Marcia Crosby, Joegh Bullock, Dori Lane, Juliet Carr, and all the others for beyond generous support after my house burned down. Betty Dodson, Susun Weed and the Wise Woman Center, Ron Athey, Texas Tomboy, and Kate Bornstein, for inspiration. The Headlands Center for the Arts for subsidizing an art studio on the beach for me. To Torch Gallery (Adriaan Van Der Have), Volitile (Peter Huttinger), Charles Lago and the R.J. Shiffler Foundation for keeping me visible in the art world. Thanks to the photographers whose photos we have utilized, and especially Dona Ann McAdams for her tremendous generosity. To each of the people we interviewed: Veronica Vera, Linda Montano, Barbara Carrellas, Richard Schechner, Mae Tyme, Monika Treut and to every person mentioned in this book. A special thanks to those I accidentally forgot to thank. I am eternally grateful to you all.

In Loving Memory of Lynda Lee Hart
(1953–2000)

Break your heart no longer. Each time you judge yourself, you break your heart. You stop feeding on the love
that is the wellspring of your vitality. But now the time
has come, your time, to live, to celebrate and to see the
goodness that you are. There is no wrong in you or any
other. There is only the thought of it, and the thought
has no substance. You are dear, divine, and very very
pure. Let no one, no thing, no ideal or idea obstruct you.
If one comes, even in the name of truth, forgive the
thought for its unknowing. Do not fight it, just let go
and breathe into the goodness that you are.

Kirpal Venanji

Introduction: Sacred Bazoombas

Gabrielle Cody

> You can never demystify a cervix.
>
> *(Annie Sprinkle)*

> Prostitute performance artists have not only transgressed public space and academic space by bringing the pornographic, the carnavalesque, into these realms, but in so doing they have produced a new social identity – the prostitute as sexual healer, goddess, teacher, political activist, and feminist – a new social identity which can trace its genealogy to the ancient sacred prostitute.
>
> *(Shannon Bell)*

When I was a little girl, I lived with my parents in the Marais district of Paris. The particular street we lived on, the rue des Rosiers, had by then become famous, a kind of unspoken memorial to the thousands of Jews who had been deported during the occupation, taken from their homes in the middle of the night, turned in by their gentile neighbors. But now – except for Goldenberg's, on the corner, and the temple, on the rue Malar – pungent Turkish bakeries and small fruit markets run by Algerians lined the neighborhood's streets. The rue des Rosiers also happened to be a popular thoroughfare for the ladies of the night returning home from work in the early hours of the morning, a baguette or two tucked under an arm.

My daily walk to the Metro St Antoine, clad in a dark-blue uniform, two uneven blond braids protruding from a thick coat collar, and with an over-laden book satchel on my back, made me an unremarkable part of the bustling morning landscape. The task at hand for this little Catholic girl, especially on gray winter mornings, was to make an invisible bee-line for the safe, warm, breathy lungs of the Metro's stairs, while ignoring the lonely taunts of street sweepers imported to France from all over the Magreb.

Separated from their families for years at a time, these men lived packed like sardines under the corrugated roofs of bidonvilles, when they weren't keeping the city's gutters clean. On one such morning, such a man stopped sweeping. He looked at me intensely, and awkwardly grabbed my unformed, uniformed breasts. Just then, a woman cut in. She spoke very quietly. She told the man that she was there for that purpose. Arab or not, Jew or not, poor or not, she was there for that reason, and to leave the girl alone. Wasn't anything sacred? She took my hand and walked me to the Metro station. This was my first encounter with the ethics of prostitution. And here I was, on my way to convent school.

Years later, at an American university, I heard about a sex labor activist turned performance artist who invited people to look at her cervix with a flashlight and marketed 'post-porn' pleasure postcards. I confess that I instantly recalled the woman who had intervened on my behalf, scaring the poor street sweeper half to death. But I also felt somewhat ashamed to have treasured for so many years the 'hooker with a heart of gold' cliché as one of my favorite childhood memories. That is, until I met Annie Sprinkle.

Annie has taught me, among other things, that autobiography – aside from being creative – is also metaphorical, and transformative. The answer to clichés is not no clichés, but better clichés, deconstructed clichés, reconstructed clichés, performative clichés. In brief, clichés that are not afraid of their past. Unlike so many borrowed words which soon turn into outmoded commodities – malaise, soupçon, frisson – the French definition of cliché is strikingly devoid of pejorative content: 'experience, image, negative, film, prototype.'[1] Annie works with and through the discarded promises of her life experiences, in the dialectical space of her cross-over from whore and porn queen to ex-mainstream porn star, post-pin-up photographer, sex worker rights activist, to trans-media artist and lesbian feminist mermaid. In the process, she also demonstrates that there is only one class of women. One of the challenges and pleasures of watching Annie's work, I think, is that it is theoretically sophisticated without appearing to be. She literally embodies theory.

Her souvenir self-portrait postcard, entitled 'Anatomy of a Pin-Up,' is a brilliant case in point. The image is of Sprinkle clad in the black corset, garter-belt stockings and high heels of the call-girl breathlessly waiting to service her client. But the joke is on the viewer. Surrounding the self-staged image of Sprinkle's voluptuous cleavage and naughty sexiness is a protuberance of graffiti-like, hand-written disclaimers such as 'Breasts are real but sag. Bra lifts breasts,' or, 'Lungs restricted I cannot breath,' or yet again, 'My feet are killing me.' As Shannon Bell explains, 'Annie makes [the] connection between all women and female porn stars and the presence of each in the same body ....'[2] Her deconstruction of the masquerade of femininity and of the performance of seduction serves to demonstrate that in commodity capitalism, there are no 'private' women.[3]

In many ways, Annie disavows mastery. Her performances imitate the direct, unmatrixed address of her burlesque years, but they also reference the hyper-intimate quality of commercial seduction. We are always reminded of our position as consumers. Indeed, we are constructed as such. Annie's paratheatrical intermissions recall the fair booths of carnival. These are occasions for her fans to – in the spirit of 'carne-vale' – valorize Annie's flesh by having their picture taken, heads framed by her coconut-sized breasts, in a 'Tits-On-The-Head Polaroid,' or to purchase one of many Sprinkle souvenirs in the form of porno prayer candles, cervix buttons, postcards, porn videos, books or Tit-Prints. She is always winking at us through these cottage-industry totems. Annie truly embodies postmodernism's roots in irony, pastiche, and unapologetic political ambiguity. Her many personas epitomize postmodernity's 'split' subject and this stance is nowhere more pronounced than in Annie's categorical refusal to be cast by anti-porn feminists in the unitary role of victim. Her performances and radical sex activism celebrate the experimental, psychically dangerous but inevitably unstable nature of identity. And this notion permeates her understanding of others too. As she wryly puts it, 'I think Andrea Dworkin is really a brilliant performance artist.'[4]

The title of her autobiography, *Annie Sprinkle, Post-Porn Modernist: My Twenty-five Years as a Multimedia Whore*, says everything about her shrewd awareness of herself as dialectical image – commodity and seller – and her recognition of the porous boundaries between art and porn, agency and objectification, the Disney-like performativity of market consumerism itself. We are all whores her title seems to imply, but some of us are having more fun. In true postmodern fashion, Annie, looking like Lily Tomlin as an evil prom queen, bursts through the book's Technicolor cover in a lime-green tutu and bunny ears, one hand waving a magic wand, the other playfully pinching her left nipple. As in her live performances, she seems to embrace the fleshy excesses and camp aesthetics of a John Waters film, exuberantly packaging herself as magical whore on the book's cover, even as she invokes the sacrality of New Age Tantric practices throughout much of her text. And this is exactly the point. The Frank Zappa quote featured above the book's title suggests with tongue-in-cheek eloquence that 'America is better for her efforts.' Indeed, Annie is a countercultural national treasure whose 'efforts' have been those of avant-garde art itself. As performance artist Frank Moore makes clear:

> avant-garde art is the way society dreams, it is the way society expands its freedom, explores the forbidden in safety, to loosen up. Society needs its dream art, just as an individual needs to dream or she/he will go insane.[5]

I. The Girl Next Door

Annie Sprinkle – née Ellen Steinberg – is the baptismal name she playfully adopted during her golden shower days as a piss artist in the Dada tradition. Annie credits her mentor Willem de Ridder, a founding member of the Fluxus movement in Europe, for encouraging her to experiment with events or action pieces and to collapse art and porn. According to Annie, her first stage shows, or happenings, were skits with De Ridder during the late 1970s, which she later developed into the performative dialogues of *Strip Speak*, and *Nurse Sprinkle's Sex Education Class*, or interventions such as *Peace in Bed*, which she and her wife Kimberly Silver performed in Australia and other countries with members of the press as active participants. More recently, Annie and other sex-positive activists and performance artists joined together for the *Liberty Love Boat* event – a collective-action piece – to protest against Giuliani's anti-commercial sex laws.

But Annie is first and foremost a raconteuse whose body is her text. As she tells the story, her journey from shy Ellen Steinberg to porn star Annie Sprinkle began at seventeen. Having just lost her virginity, Ellen left her family in suburban Southern California, and landed a job at the Plaza Cinema in Tucson, Arizona. There she sold popcorn for $4.75 an hour during runs of one of the most successful porno flicks of the 1970s, Gerard Damiano's *Deep Throat*. That is, until the movie house was busted and closed down. After her ill-fated job at the Plaza, Ellen began working the phones at the North Star, a three-bedroom mobile home which housed a 'full-body' massage business. It took Annie one afternoon to realize which end of the business really paid. But it took Ellen considerably longer to comprehend the negative societal connotations surrounding her lucrative and pleasurable work. As Annie puts it:

> I was working as a prostitute for a good two months before I realized it! When it finally did occur to me ... I enjoyed the idea. It wasn't at all like the nightmare depicted on TV or in the movies.[6]

Elsewhere, she further challenges puritanical assumptions about prostitution. As Sheila Marie Thomas suggests:

> Sprinkle arrived at the role of prostitute indirectly, thus subverting its power. Rather than consciously having sex with strangers for money, she had sex with them for fun. When she realized that her actions personified her as whore in the eyes of society, she chose to actively accept the role. Claiming it as her own identity in the moment of recognition, she says she 'enjoyed the idea' of calling herself a hooker.[7]

Her identity as whore began as a performance. Linda Williams also points to Sprinkle's prostitution as a form of agency:

> In this first instance of sexual performance in which [Sprinkle] first wasn't, and then was, 'hailed' as a whore, we can see the discovery of an agency that is not opposed to, but rooted in, the discourse that constructs her. Her agency could be said to consist in the fact that in the repetition of the performance of sex, first for free, then for money, she realizes that 'whore' does not fully name who she is. Annie Sprinkle neither denies that she is a whore nor fights the system that so names her.[8]

But Marla Carlson rightly maintains that Williams

> does not take full account of Sprinkle's rhetorical construction of her life story. [Williams] treats the story as a representation of Sprinkle's experience. As representation it doesn't ring true. As a performative act, however, the story effects a transformation.[9]

Like Genet, who, according to Sartre, defied bourgeois morality by performing the status of thief/homosexual and saint – thereby queering his own criminality by 'owning' it – Annie's performative whoredom was imbued with a psychedelic sense of political communitas, the civil disobedience of a counter-culture at the height of the sexual revolution of the 1970s. The story of her arrival in New York six months after the forced closing of *Deep Throat* is as fantasmatic as the movie itself. Annie was served a subpoena to appear in court, where she was asked by authorities to identify her employers. During the proceedings, she met Damiano and Linda Lovelace, the film's heroine, whose clitoris is magically located in her throat. As Sprinkle remembers it, she asked Damiano to teach her how to 'deep throat' and followed him back to Manhattan. But what she learned through her apprenticeship was more than how to give a great blow job.

In New York, Sprinkle became an apprentice at Kirt Studios, a low-budget hardcore feature film factory. Though she at first declined to be in Leonard Kirtman's features, because, as she puts it, 'I thought one day I might want to be an art teacher,'[10] she eventually tired of working behind the scenes. By the mid-1970s she had starred in over a hundred porn flicks including such vivid and now kitsch titles as *Teenage Masseuse, Centerfold Fever, Wet Christmas, Slippery When Wet, Teenage Deviate, Kneel before Me*, and *The Devil Inside Her*. She also worked as a pin-up model for *Stag, Cheri, High Society, Chic*, and *Hustler*, as well as lesser-known publications like *Foot Fetish Times, Enema News*, and *Sluts and Slobs*. A major turning point came in 1978, when she met Willem de Ridder, who, along with artists such as Shigeko Kubota, George Maciunas, and Yoshiko Chumo, became important role models. After working together on an alternative sex magazine pithily named *Love*, they eloped to Italy for a year and a half. De Ridder, to whom she dedicates her autobiography, had a monumental influence on Annie's development as a mono-printer, photographer and conceptual artist: in brief, for her passage from porn to 'post-porn,' 'object' to 'subject.' Annie and de Ridder edited *The Sprinkle Report, the Newsletter Devoted to Piss Art*, fittingly published by the R. Mutt Press. But Sprinkle's cottage-industry sales, the Sprinkle Salon mail-order business 'Golden Shower Ritual Kits' – featuring small bottles of urine – derived strongly from George Maciunas's humorous send-up of porno-fetish venture capitalism, and his Fluxus Mail-Order Warehouse concept. Similarly, during the 1980s pieces like Sprinkle's *Post-Porn Modernist* show would draw from Fluxus artists who had previously focused on race and sex, and whose work had strong proto-feminist influences. Sprinkle's infamous 'Public Cervix Announcement' is in direct lineage with both Yoko Ono's 1964 performance entitled 'Cut Piece,' 'in which [Ono] sat motionless on the stage after inviting the audience to come up and cut away her clothing . . .'[11] and Shigeko Kubota's 1965 'Vagina Painting' performance, in which she applied paint to paper using a brush inserted into her vagina. After graduating from the School of Visual Arts in Manhattan with a BA in Fine Arts, Annie worked in the High-Heel School of Journalism with Veronica Vera as photographer for most of the magazines she had previously posed for, as well as mainstream publications such as *Newsweek*, documenting the sex scene in the 1980s.

Nineteen eighty-one was another turning point in Annie's journey. This was the year she wrote and directed her own feature film, *Deep Inside Annie Sprinkle*, which opened at the World Theater in New York City. At a later screening in a gigantic drive-in movie theater in Akron, Ohio, and with quintessential Sprinkle panache, Annie, as mistress of ceremonies, hosted the event by addressing the 900 cars of spectators over loudspeakers, inviting them to honk and blink their lights.

Deep Inside is a subversive queering of the hardcore norm in which women are compliant and passive. As Annie recalls:

> my concept was to make the movie interactive. I involved the viewer by talking directly into the camera. My favorite scene conceptually was one in which I go into a movie theater where one of my porn movies is playing and have sex with several of the porn fans who are watching me on screen. I also did a very intense masturbation scene, while looking into the camera, and had long multiple orgasms during which I ejaculated (although at the time we didn't know what it was). The film also had a beautifully done golden shower scene, which was later censored by the distributor to avoid legal problems.[12]

As a number of feminist scholars have observed, in *Deep Inside Annie Sprinkle*, Annie deliberately plays with the conventions of who gives pleasure to whom.[13] Much has been written about her incorporation of homosexual pornography, through her on-screen interactions with men, or what Chris Straayer has referred to as the re-inscription of sodomy into heterosexuality. But perhaps the most radical aspect of Sprinkle's performance, as Linda Williams notes, is that she distorts the physical proximity between hooker and customer by employing the 'rhetoric of intimate address to the client who is no longer there. . . . She injects elements of the narrative that disrupt the active male, passive female paradigm of conventional pornography.'[14] According to Thomas, another element in the film's scenario is striking. Sprinkle deliberately inveighs against the rarefied, isolated fantasy setting of commercial pornography:

> Once Sprinkle has invited the viewer 'into' her house, she displays her personal photo album which contains photos of herself as a child and a young woman. Rather than allowing her 'client' to assume that her glamorous whore persona is the real, original woman, the photos foreground the constructed nature of her identity; her spoken text also reminds the viewer that it is Sprinkle, rather than the (presumably male) audience, who has the power to cause this transformation from nice girl to hooker as she recites her story of Ellen Steinberg becoming Annie Sprinkle.[15]

Deep Inside Annie Sprinkle, the second best-selling adult video of 1982, not only established Annie as a Porn Star, it also marked the beginning of a tradition of direct address and interactive locution, in which the boundaries between life and art are deliberately blurred. But the film also occasioned an important personal transformation. As she says, 'I got tired of being other people's fantasy.'[16] She considered offers to do burlesque shows. But Annie's idea of burlesque had a twist, or what has been referred to as avant-garde burlesque, a strand which parodies the genre. Not coincidentally, her first performance piece was entitled *Strip Speak*, a combination of teasing rhetorical questions and commentary meant to sexually entice her male audience, while subversively sending up a whole tradition of voyeurism.

From this point on, Annie became more and more politicized, 'performing' herself as hooker and disrupting assumptions about the performance of prostitution. The scenario of her next piece, *Deep Inside Porn Stars*, came out of Club 90, a porn-star support group which started at Annie's salon and then rotated to the other members' homes. In January 1984, a feminist performance group, Carnival Knowledge, approached Sprinkle and her sister porn stars Veronica Vera, Candida Royalle, Gloria Leonard, Veronica Hart, Sue Nero and Kelly Nichols to ask them if they would consider being part of a performance series entitled *The Second Coming* at the Franklin Furnace. The program stated the aim of the series, which was to 'explore a new definition of pornography, one that is not demeaning to women, men and children.'[17] Thomas aptly describes the significance of this performance:

> Set in a replica of Annie Sprinkle's living room, the piece focused on the difference between the women's images and their 'real' selves. While the women 'gather for the meeting,' they inconspicuously remove their porn costumes, exchanging them for street clothing. [As] Bell remarks, 'the stripping, subtle as it is, connects the audience visually to burlesque theater, reminding the spectators that most of the women worked and work stripping in these theaters.' In violation of this pornographic context, Sprinkle serves tea and cookies to each woman as she arrives.[18]

That same year, after happening upon her *Nurse Sprinkle's Sex Education* show, with his NYU class on illicit theater, Richard Schechner asked Annie if she would perform her Nurse Sprinkle routine from Show World's Triple Treat Theater as part of *Prometheus Project*. His fascination with her work came from the notion that 'at each increment of sexual opportunity, Sprinkle interviews the spectator asking him to describe what he sees, or how he feels. This automatically distances the action from its own sexual possibilities – making it anti-porn or a send up of porn.'[19] Annie's acceptance of both the Franklin Furnace engagement and Schechner's invitation to include her strip show performance in 'legitimate' fringe art space provided her with a formal entrée into New York's emerging performance art scene.

As commercial sex work became less compelling, Annie increasingly sought the mentorship and encouragement of artists. When Annie met Linda Montano, who refers to herself as a 'lifeist,' one of Montano's most influential meditations on the art of/in everyday life involved living for an entire year attached by a six-foot rope to fellow artist Teching Hsieh. In 1988, Sprinkle and Veronica Vera attended Montano's Summer Saint Camp at the Art/Life Institute in Kingston, New York, where Sprinkle was, as she proudly puts it, 'baptized as an artist.' Annie speaks of her encounter with Montano as something akin to a 'religious experience.'[20] Their friendship and collaboration eventually led to many performances over the course of fourteen years, and to sexuality workshops entitled Sacred Sex, facilitated at the Wise Woman Center for a decade. Annie's more experimental, metamorphosexual docudramas of this period reflect

One of several incarnations of 'Nurse Sprinkle'; this one at a benefit for
Performance Space 122 in New York. Photo: © Dona Ann McAdams.

her shift from porn to art. *Linda/Les & Annie – The First Female-to-Male Transexual Love Story* documents her love affair with Les Nichols, a female-to-male transsexual, and surgically made hermaphrodite. The *Sluts and Goddesses Video Workshop*, marketed as 'an eye fuck,' is a humorous exploration of female sexuality and sensual pleasures, which Annie claims to have made to gain entry into the lesbian world. Today, Annie considers herself an activist, a teacher and sexual healer and trans-media artist. Her more recent work is, in her words, 'feminist, spiritual, transgendered and queer.'[21]

II. Postmodern Popcorn

Annie popularized the term 'Post-Porn' on the occasion of her 1989 one-woman show, which originated as a series of vignettes that she had performed around New York since 1981. In later incarnations, the piece became known as *Post-Post-Porn Modernist*. As in cabaret arts, each scene or number forms a discrete entity, but taken in sequence, the show traces Annie's life story from the days of shy Ellen Steinberg, through her early years as porn starlet, to the burlesque years of her Nurse Sprinkle act, to her healing work as New Age Tantric High priestess. In one of *Post-Porn Modernist*'s most notorious numbers, 'A Public Cervix Announcement,' Annie self-inserted a speculum and invited her audience to line up and view her cervix with a flashlight. As Bell notes:

> the piece cuts through the very premise of pornography – the distanced and anonymous viewer appropriating the object of desire for (usually) his pleasure. Objectifying eroticism is stripped away and in its place is eroticism of the whole female sexual organ that belongs to the subject: Annie.[22]

Her 'public cervix' piece also deconstructed an entire tradition of culturally coercive perspectivalism. Schneider describes Annie's triumph this way:

> Sprinkle spectators line up to get a peek at the scene of her cervix embedded in her exposed pussy, which is in turn embedded in her specific body, kinkily clothed in the raiment of a porn queen. The body, on a bed raked for visibility, is embedded on the stage of The Kitchen, which is an art space embedded in the tradition of the avant-garde, embedded in the larger frame of the

Annie Sprinkle at the end of the 100 Blow Jobs scene in *Post-Porn Modernist*. Photo: © Dona Ann McAdams.

art establishment, embedded in the ideals of Western history, a history of a patriarchy which, broadly speaking, can be said to be embedded in the effort to manipulate and control ... the scene of the cervix.[23]

In an earlier vignette called 'Pornstistics' Annie displayed a series of computerized pie charts and graphs, while gleefully interrogating her most basic motivations for being a hooker with such titles as 'Why I Did It: Advantages,' or 'Why I Did It: Disadvantages.' After weighing both perspectives, she concludes unsentimentally that the Pros have outweighed the Cons. But not by far. In true Brechtian fashion, Sprinkle reveals that economic relations determine human choices. As Bell suggests, Annie's calculations are hilariously blunt:

A bar graph depicts the 'Amount of cock sucked' by juxtaposing a penis to the Empire State Building; placed end to end the former equals the latter minus the antenna. A second bar graph compares Annie's weekly income of $4,000 [as a feature stripper] to an average American woman's weekly income of $243; the final bar graph makes the difference in income wider by comparing Annie's seventeen-hour workweek to the forty-hour workweek. [But] just as the audience is either beginning to think that the benefits of pornography/prostitution outweigh the drawbacks ... Annie enacts '100 Blow Jobs,' in which she performs fellatio on a dozen dildos nailed to a board while male voices on a taped soundtrack make angry demands. The segment does not end in humiliation, as one would expect, but rather, with Annie sitting at her make-up table and giving herself the Aphrodite Award for sexual service to the community. She expresses her life-sex philosophy: 'we are ALL sexually abused by virtue of the fact that we live in a sex-negative society.'[24]

The 'post' that Annie reaches for toward the end of the show is that of the ancient sacred prostitute, a healer and teacher. Bare-breasted, and vibrator in hand, Annie invokes the myth of the ancient temple and re-creates a masturbation ritual in which she asks her audience to accompany her building sexual ecstasy by shaking rattles handed out by ushers, in order to take prayers to the divine realm.

But Annie's complication of the power relations inherent in representational acts – the 'exploded' theatrical viewing of the

Annie Sprinkle invokes 'The Legend of the Ancient Sacred Prostitute' in *Post-Porn Modernist*. Photo: © Dona Ann McAdams.

explicit body as it were – raises important theoretical issues. Her 'post-porn' pornography finds its inspiration in radical feminism's somewhat romanticized notion of an ancient, matriarchal-sacred, as well as the confrontationalism of high modernism. As Schneider suggests, 'Sprinkle is problematically emblematic' of 'the messy impasse between essentialist and constructivist critiques of gender' because '[while] she presents her identity as masquerade, she looks to her profession as "holy".'[25] Annie confirms this perspective in speaking of her *Post-Porn Modernist* show: 'I really think that the masturbation ritual was the most interesting performance, much more so than the public cervix announcement.'[26] At the same time, though, Annie has a highly sophisticated relationship to the performative dimensions of mediated duplication as a means toward subjecthood. Her most recent performance piece, *Annie Sprinkle's Herstory of Porn – From Reel to Real* juxtaposes footage of Annie in dozens of porn flicks with her live presence on stage inhabiting a multitude of clichéd personas ranging from horny bimbette to teenage deviate, to S/M mistress, to fringe artist, to New Age lesbian sex guru. These figures are metaphors for all the different phases in (her) evolution and they confirm Chris Straayer's contention that in Annie's 'autobiographical artwork[s], ... self-actualization relies on artifice as much as origins.'[27] As Annie puts it, 'this is my Forrest Gump story. An ideal dream would be if Woody Allen could do a Hollywood version of this story.'[28]

One way to reconcile Annie's stance as materialist and cultural feminist is to explore the dialectical relationship of her autobiographical journey from 'reel' to 'real.' Though Annie's sexual formation was steeped in what Williams refers to as in the 'will-to-knowledge/power' of Western *scientia sexualis*[29] which underlies the ethos of hardcore pornography, Sprinkle eventually borrowed heavily from Eastern *ars erotica* philosophies which instead 'aim[ed] at passing general knowledge from the experienced to the initiate.'[30] As Williams notes:

> In *The History of Sexuality* Michel Foucault distinguishes between two primary ways of organizing the knowledge of sexuality. Where ancient and non-Western cultures had organized the knowledge of sex around an erotic art, or *ars erotica*, ... without specifying or classifying the details of this knowledge, modern Western cultures have increasingly constructed a *scientia sexualis*

– hermeneutics of desire aimed at ever more detailed explorations of the scientific truths of sexuality. The *scientia sexualis*, Foucault argues, constructs modern sexualities according to a conjunction of power and knowledge that probes the measurable, confessable 'truths' of a sexuality that governs bodies and their pleasures.[31]

While Annie may spoof the principles of *scientia sexualis* in pieces like her *Nurse Sprinkle's Sex Education Class*, and to some extent in 'A Public Cervix Announcement,' she seems genuinely to embrace the mystical expansiveness of *ars erotica* philosophies. Her contention that you can never demystify a cervix recalls the Great Mother mythos, and so too does her masturbation ritual. Still, rather than awkwardly straddling an essentialist and materialist impasse, Annie succeeds in fusing the two, making her, in effect, an anti-essentialist essentialist.

The title of her latest performance piece, *Herstory of Porn – From Reel to Real*, in many ways dramatizes the historical importance and subversive potential of alternative feminist porn which is interactive, humorous and spiritually therapeutic, since it is meant to heal and educate far more than to arouse. In a seven-part scenario, which Annie parallels with the seven Chakras,[32] Sprinkle documents her twenty-five years in the porn and post-porn industry, and her passage from *scientia sexualis* to *ars erotica*, from pornography's traditional 'frenzy of the visible' – a dramaturgy that invariably culminates with the 'cum-shot' or 'money-shot' of an ejaculating penis – to more sensory, less scopic and less realistic genres of porn. Sprinkle watches herself perform in dozens of hardcore flicks and chronicles in wry Brechtian fashion her evolution from porn star apprentice to docu-pornographer, always with a keen awareness that even as the star-hostess of her own New Age porno films, she is unrepresentable except as representation.[33] But also with an understanding that her performance necessitates a degree of shamanistic suffering.

In many ways, *Herstory of Porn* – which was directed by longtime friend and collaborator Emilio Cubeiro in 1999 and performed in San Francisco, New York, Chicago, Ohio, and Texas, as well as France and Holland, is 'vintage' Sprinkle. As always, Annie maintains an ironic distance from her performance and is utterly in control of the means of production. But this time, she not only hosts her own presence on stage but also that of her Double, presented through the mediated duplication of her younger celluloid self in a series of hardcore film clips. An earlier version of *Herstory*, entitled *Hardcore from the Heart*, featured a similar conceit, but lacked the sophistication and incisiveness of Cubeiro's staging. If the on-screen portion of *Herstory* demonstrates the clichéd mechanics of hardcore pornography in which men act and women appear, Annie on stage explores the politics and metaphysics of her cross-over from porn to art, youth to maturity, heterosexuality to metamorphosexuality. *Herstory* is not a performance in the traditional sense, as much as it is the ritual transformation Annie has invited us to witness: the rugged journey through many different identity politics.

P.S. 122, where *Herstory* was performed when I saw it during the late spring of 1999, is transformed into a porno movie house complete with two functional popcorn concession stands on either side of the stage framing a row of theater seats. Behind these seats is a movie screen flanked by curtains. Over the course of the piece, Annie takes us to the Pink Pussy Cat Sinema (Hollywood), Mitchell Brothers Theatre (San Francisco), the Orleans Theater (New York City), the New Age Sex Multiplex (Taos, New Mexico), the Museum of Modern Art (New York City), the Sappho Film Co-op (Northampton, Massachusetts), and back to Performance Space 122, New York City, where Annie comes full circle, 'to a place of compassion and acceptance.'[34]

But *Herstory* is also one of Annie's boldest efforts as a trans-media artist at creative autobiographical risk-taking. The dramatic tension of the piece comes from the multi-layered juxtaposition of Annie's 'reel'/fetishized images on screen, those produced by the porn-industry apparatus, and her equally artificial personas on stage speaking back to the frames that produced her as porn star. The most radical element of this event is not the pornographic content of the clips Annie shows us, but rather, the boldness and vulnerability of the speech acts she performs alongside. Similarly, the plurivocity of her narrative – what Marla Carlson refers to as 'the variety of speech communities within which she operates'[35] – creates fascinating audience proxemics. Annie's audience is composed of old porn fans from her burlesque years, suburban couples who recently saw her HBO *Real Sex* appearances, feminist academics and practitioners and other sex workers, and a younger pro-sex, pro-pornography generation of female fans who are studying her work in universities.

This is ultimately what makes Annie such a compelling subject: her desire and ability to dream consciously, and to bring such vastly different constituencies together and risk the clichés of our differences. My sense is that an artist who makes her cervix and 'Bosom Ballet' available to viewers on the Web, and vibrates her double on stage, not only has a fabulous sense of humor in the tradition of Jarry and Duchamp but also a wider understanding of the pornographic culture of information technology itself. Annie's post-porn modernism is a way of grappling with the meaning of the live female body in this techno-cultural moment, the era of simulation and virtual gratification, and of dismantling old paradigms and hierarchies of pleasure.

And she does have a heart of gold.

Notes

1. Henri Bertaud du Chazaud, *Nouveau Dictionnaire des synonymes* (Paris: Hachette-Tchou, 1971), p. 427.
2. Shannon Bell, *Reading, Writing and Rewriting the Prostitute Body* (Bloomington and Indianapolis: Indiana University Press, 1994), p. 149.
3. Rebecca Schneider, *The Explicit Body in Performance* (London and New York: Routledge, 1997), p. 51.
4. Annie Sprinkle, 'Risk and vulnerability – fixing taboos,' flyer handed out by Annie during visiting artist presentations.
5. Quoted in *ibid.*
6. Annie Sprinkle, *Annie Sprinkle: Post-Porn Modernist: My Twenty-five Years as a Multimedia Whore* (San Francisco: Cleis Press, 1998), p. 25.
7. Sheila Marie Thomas, 'Speaking the Unspeakable: Annie Sprinkle's "Prostitute Performances"' (master's thesis: University of Colorado, 1996), p. 6.
8. Linda Williams, *Hard Core: Power, Pleasure and the 'Frenzy of the Visible'* (Berkeley: University of California Press, 1999), p. 180.
9. Marla Carlson, 'Performative pornography: Annie Sprinkle reads her movies,' *Text and Performance Quarterly*, 19 (July 1999), p. 239.
10. Sprinkle, *Post-Porn Modernist*, p. 27.
11. Kristine Stiles, 'Between water and stone,' in Elizabeth Armstrong and Joan Rothfuss (eds), *In the Spirit of Fluxus* (Minneapolis: Walker Art Center, 1993), p. 81.
12. Sprinkle, *Post-Porn Modernist*, pp. 33–4.
13. Williams, *Hard Core*, pp. 184–5.
14. *Ibid.*, pp. 181, 184.
15. Thomas, 'Speaking the Unspeakable,' p. 9.
16. *Ibid.*, p. 12.
17. Bell, *Prostitute Body*, p. 143.
18. Thomas, 'Speaking the Unspeakable,' p. 13.
19. *Ibid.*, p. 15.

20. Annie Sprinkle, interview with the author, Poughkeepsie, New York, April 2000.
21. *Ibid.*
22. Bell, *Prostitute Body*, p. 152.
23. Schneider, *Explicit Body in Performance*, p. 60.
24. Bell, *Prostitute Body*, p. 151.
25. Schneider, *Explicit Body in Performance*, pp. 53, 58.
26. Sprinkle, interview with the author.
27. Chris Straayer, *Deviant Eyes, Deviant Bodies: Sexual Re-orientation in Film and Video* (New York: Columbia University Press, 1996), p. 156.
28. Sprinkle, interview with the author.
29. Williams, *Hard Core*, p. 48.
30. *Ibid.*
31. *Ibid.*, p. 34.
32. Sprinkle, interview with the author.
33. Schneider, *Explicit Body in Performance*, p. 22.
34. Sprinkle, interview with the author.
35. Carlson, 'Performative pornography,' p. 239.

Part I

Actions, Rituals, Performances

Strip Speak: Nurse Sprinkle's Sex Education Class

(As presented in Richard Schechner's *Prometheus Project*)

In the early 1980s, porn stars were suddenly in high demand at burlesque theaters. I was getting offers I couldn't refuse to take it all off, live on stage. My boyfriend and art mentor at the time, Willem de Ridder, suggested that I tell erotic stories on stage. Being a creative kind of gal, but not being a very good dancer, this was a perfect idea. We called our new genre of burlesque 'Strip Speak.' I hit the bumpy burlesque trail.

   I created several skits which I mostly improvised while I was interacting with the (almost always all-male and sometimes masturbating) audience. Eventually I ended up doing a collaborative version of my Nurse Sprinkle skit in an Off-Off Broadway theater performance directed by Richard Schechner called the *Prometheus Project* (1985). This was the perfect bridge for me to cross over into the high-brow theater world. Being quite shy, I'm certain I never would have had the courage to go on stage and do a one-woman show in an art venue if I hadn't had this basic stage experience in strip clubs. Here is an excerpt from Richard Schechner's script.

ANNIE: Hi boys and girls, welcome to Nurse Sprinkle's Sex Education Class. Now I know that some of you out there already know a little about the birds and the bees, but most of you look like virgins to me. Are you virgins?

(ANNIE nods 'yes' to coax spectators to nod 'yes.' Some always do. Throughout her scene, ANNIE always treats the audience with great, exaggerated respect. And whenever she reacts to what they do she does so in an over-the-top way.)

OK. So we are going to go over these important facts of life here in class today. What it's all about is when a boy meets a girl *(slide of line drawing of boy meets girl)* . . . and when they like each other a lot,

they get this overwhelming desire to do what is called 'make love.'
They want to press their lips together and slide their eager tongues
into each other's mouths. This is called 'french kissing' *(slide)*.
Then they want to press their bodies together and give each other
big, hard hugs.

Let's try a class experiment. Who wants to try a big hug?
(ANNIE actively goes into the audience to find participants.) You do? OK.
Just wrap your arms around me like this . . . good . . . squeeze hard
. . . ummmph . . . yeah. Isn't that nice?

*(ANNIE puts the microphone near the participant's mouth – she interviews
him/her even while the person is in the act of hugging. After the spectator
says something, ANNIE goes on. Sometimes she improvises dialog with the
spectators.)*

Let's all give this student a great big hand. *(Audience applauds.)*
That was an excellent hug. This brings us to a most important
topic. Tits! These are tits. I have two tits. Let's all count them
together. Ooooonnne, twwwoooo! *(ANNIE's two assistants flash
their breasts.)* I didn't hear you. Louder. OK, again, Ooooonnne,
twwwooo! That's better. Very good. Hey, would you boys and
girls like to see a pair of tits for real right here in class? Would
you? OK, I'll show you mine. *(Someone in the audience helps ANNIE
take off her nurse's dress. Then she pulls her bra to the side revealing a
nipple.)* This spot here is called the niiipppplllle. Can you all say
that? All together now: 'niiipppplllle.' *(ANNIE pinches her nipple a
little, and sighs.)* Ooohh, you're a wonderful class. You're so smart!
Now when the male and the female are making love the nipples
become very, very, very sensitive when they are touched. Let's see
what happens when the male touches the female nipple. *(ANNIE
selects someone from the audience to touch her nipple.)* Just put your fingers on it . . . good, rub it, maybe pinch it a little, yessss,
oooohhhh, ahhhh, yeah! Let's give this man a big hand. *(Audience
applauds.)* Now, let's examine the nipple a little more carefully. Do
you boys and girls see what happened there? My nipple got all hard
like a pebble. Isn't that fascinating? Let's take a look at what the
rest of a pair of titties looks like. Who wants to help me take off
my bra? *(Spectator unhooks bra. Meanwhile the audience to the side, the
CHORUS, consisting of performers dressed in raincoats, are simulating masturbating.)* Now I'll just let my big, bulbous boobies dangle free.
The female's titties just love to be massaged and caressed by a nice
pair of strong hands. . . . Who would like to try that? *(ANNIE picks*

a man or woman in the audience.) Go ahead, put one hand here and one hand there and roll them around . . . yes, that's it . . . Hey, are you sure that this is your first time? You do that so well! Let's give him [or her] a big hand. That was excellent. A+.

Now we come to something especially interesting. No one can explain why, but for some reason the male loves to wrap a woman's titties tightly around his head. Who would like to try that? (*ANNIE picks a man wearing glasses and wraps her breasts around his head.*) You'd better take off your glasses first. Good. Put your face in there and . . . that's it. Isn't that nice? What does it feel like. (*ANNIE puts the microphone to the man to get an answer – which is usually muffled.*) Can you actually breathe down there? Let's give him a big hand!

The next topic is very, very important. It's where to kiss the female. (*A slide comes up with dozens of tiny red arrows pointing to many spots around the female body; but there is a close-up of the genitals.*) Now as you can see from the diagram, just about every spot likes to be kissed with a pair of warm, loving lips, but when making love there is an area that is particularly sensitive. Can any of you students guess what that is? No, it's not the elbow . . . take another guess. No, it's not the toes. Give up? OK, it's the area right between the female's legs – this area here called the 'love hole.' Can you all say that with me? Looooovvvvvve hoolllllle. Very good. Hey? Would you boys and girls like to see what a love hole looks like for real? OK. I'll show you mine. (*Assistants bring ANNIE a magnifying glass and a flashlight.*) Let's look at it under the microscope. (*She hands the glass and the light to a spectator.*) I'll pull my panties down and spread my lips so you can get a nice close look. There, can you see it? Don't be afraid. You can get much closer than that. Closer. How does it look? Can you describe my love hole to the people in the back who can't see it from where they are sitting? (*ANNIE puts the microphone to the person's mouth for the description, which is usually pretty funny. Here ANNIE improvises depending on the response she gets from the spectator.*) Very good. Let's give this eager student a big hand. That was an excellent description. Another A+.

Our next topic here in class today is the male genital area (*slide*), which is located between the male's legs. This part is called the 'love pole.' Can you all say that with me? Loooooovvvve poooolllllllle. Good! The male likes to have his love pole played with while making love. Now this may come as a big shock to many of you, and you may even find it thoroughly disgusting, but the female sometimes likes to suck on the male's love pole. Who would like to volunteer their love pole for a little demonstration of cock sucking? *(Usually no one volunteers, at least in artsy crowds.)* Nobody?? OK, I'll demonstrate on the class dummy. *(Assistants bring out a big dildo.)* Now, I like to get down on my knees, and the man stands up in front of me, and I start by gently stroking and caressing his love pole. *(ANNIE demonstrates on the dildo. As she demonstrates the CHORUS gets more and more excited, finally climaxing and throwing crumpled kleenexes out onto the stage.)* Then I look up into his eyes and I tell him how much I love and adore him and how wonderful and sexy he is . . . that's very important . . . then I gently plant a big kiss right on the love pole's head.

(Just as ANNIE is about to kiss the dildo all the lights in the theater come up brightly. ANNIE and all the performers stare at the spectators. The DIRECTOR, carrying a camera, walks slowly out into the performing area and begins to take pictures of the spectators. The lights remain on very bright for about 30–45 seconds. When the bright lights go off and the theater lights come on again and ANNIE is about to begin sucking, the MC comes on.)

Metamorphosexual MudBath Ritual: A Private Performance

Artist Linda Montano introduced me to the idea of 'life as art' and taught me that a performance doesn't necessarily require a live audience. An artist can do a 'private performance.'

Here is a script for a private performance, which I invite anyone who is interested to perform. This was inspired by an exercise that my friend and Tantra teacher Jwala taught me. It's a good one to do once a year or so. It will be different each time.

Ingredients:

1 bath tub (the larger the better)
$\frac{1}{2}$ cup flower petals
1 stick of incense
1 candle
1 matchbook or lighter
3 sea shells
$\frac{1}{2}$ cup scented bath oil
1 package beauty clay (available in health food and beauty supply stores)
Dental floss
Gum stimulator (the rubber tip found on most toothbrushes)
Your favorite pajamas
Pen and paper
Scotch tape

1. Put your answering machine on so you don't have to answer your telephone.
2. Go into your bathroom, close the door and run a hot bath. Sprinkle flower petals and scented bath oil into the water to help make this a special, ritual bath. Drop sea shells in the water to bring in the healing and erotic powers of the ocean.
3. Light a stick of incense to stimulate your sense of smell and purify the atmosphere in the bathroom with smoke. Light a candle and then turn out all the lights.

4. Stand in front of your mirror and apply the beauty mud all over your body, face and hair. Do this slowly and sensuously, enjoying the messiness and sexiness of the sensations. Make it erotic.

5. Sit on the toilet. Poop and/or pee if desired. Spend the next few minutes meditating on your own personal sexual evolution. Where have you come from? What have you done or not done? What role has sexuality played in your life? What are your best sexual skills? In what areas are you weak? What have you learned and what more do you want to learn? Think about the good times and the bad times. Focus all your attention on reviewing your sex life up to the present. In your mind's eye, watch the porn movie of your own life. Acknowledge this point in time.

6. Now slowly slip into the bath tub. You must not do any normal bath chores like washing your hair, shaving or scrubbing your nails. Your purpose is simply to relax and luxuriate in the sensations.

7. Close your eyes. Let go. Try floating on both your back and front. Congratulate yourself for all your sexual accomplishments, and for making it as far as you have. Give yourself love. Let yourself surrender into an erotic vibratory state. Surrender your will to the pleasure and the subtle ecstasy energy in the universe that's available just for the asking.

8. Imagine that you are a fetus floating in a womb. Remember the feeling of safety and also the feeling of total sensual immersion.

9. Now open the bath tub drain, but remain in the tub as the water flows out of the drain. Imagine that as the water level goes down, you are being born again as a whole new you. Imagine that the muddy water that flows away contains any thoughts and feelings which have kept you from enjoying your full pleasure potential. Celebrate the beginning of the rest of your life.

10. Shower off the rest of the clay. Don't worry about cleaning the tub. You can do that tomorrow.

11. Gently towel yourself dry. Let it be erotic.

12. Brush and floss your teeth. Use a rubber tip on your gums. Clean your ears, and blow your nose if desired. Put on your favorite pajamas.

13. Now write a list of the ten things that bring you the most

pleasure in your life such as swimming, dancing, making love, getting a massage, riding a Harley Davidson, fishing, shopping, writing poetry ... etc.

14. Think about how much time you spend doing these things. Is it a lot, a little, or none at all? How can you transform your life to spend even more time doing the things you love most?

15. Tape this list on your mirror so you can refer to it regularly. If you want a happy, pleasure-filled life, you now have a clear list of the things you can do to have it.

16. Go do at least one of the things on your list.

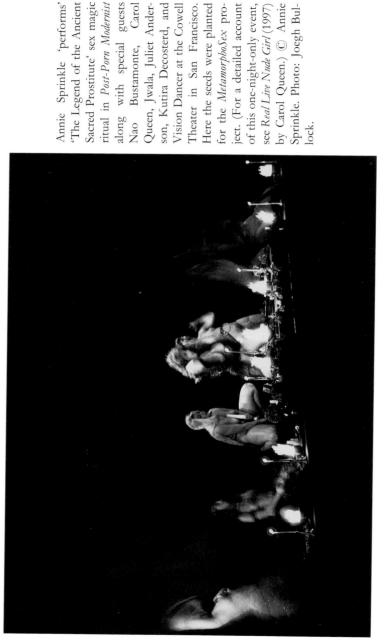

Annie Sprinkle 'performs' 'The Legend of the Ancient Sacred Prostitute' sex magic ritual in *Post-Porn Modernist* along with special guests Nao Bustamonte, Carol Queen, Jwala, Juliet Anderson, Kutira Decosterd, and Vision Dancer at the Cowell Theater in San Francisco. Here the seeds were planted for the *MetamorphoSex* project. (For a detailed account of this one-night-only event, see *Real Live Nude Girl* (1997) by Carol Queen.) © Annie Sprinkle. Photo: Joegh Bullock.

MetamorphoSex

When I performed *Post-Porn Modernist*, for five years around the world, the show always climaxed with a sex magic masturbation ritual I called 'The Legend of the Ancient Sacred Prostitute.' I learned and experienced more from doing that piece than anything else I have ever done in my life, and many people told me they were inspired or touched by it. I wished that everyone could have the intense experience of going into ecstasy on stage in a theatrical setting. So, I invited six friends to do the 'Legend of the Sacred Prostitute' masturbation ritual along with me in a show at the elegant Cowell Theater in San Francisco. A year later, I did it with sixteen friends, also at the Cowell. We incorporated the erotic massage techniques that Joseph Kramer and I had developed, and the Big Draw (a Taoist technique which creates an energetic climax). The ritual was only about twenty minutes long. With more women involved, it felt way too short. I wanted to explore the concepts more, go deeper into the experience, and make it more of a theater piece. But how?

The MetamorphoSex concept was born in a eureka-type moment with Barbara Carrellas and Linda Montano, my dear friends with whom I had taught and performed Sacred Sexuality workshops for years. MetamorphoSex became a workshop, sex magic ritual and theater performance rolled into one. It premiered at the Vortex Repertory Theater in Austin, Texas, in December 1995. At Linda's suggestion, we have now changed the name to The Art of Love. Eventually, we hope to tour it around the USA and Europe, perhaps with a core group traveling around in a caravan of mobile homes. Presently we are doing it with women participants only. In the future, there might be a second week for men (with male facilitators). And a third week for all genders together.

First, we put out a flyer inviting women to participate. We then follow the basic structure presented here. However, as the cultural and personal needs of the three of us change, and as our collaborators change, the format and structure of The Art of Love changes. Love is our goal, unconditional love for our temple-bodies and tolerance and compassion for all beings. We may even do Art of Love workshops/performances in the future that won't look like sex at all.

METAMORPHOSEX – THE ART OF LOVE
A SACRED SEX WORKSHOP & THREE RITUAL PERFORMANCES

'Our sexuality is not only something that can be used for the enhancement of an intimate relationship, for physical pleasure or procreation; it can also be used for personal transformation, physical and emotional healing, self-realization, spiritual growth, and as a way to learn about all of life . . . and death. An honest, focused, sexually knowledgeable and supportive group of women is a divine and extremely powerful force that can not only inspire each woman in that group, but has the potential to contribute to the well-being of all life on earth.'

Annie Sprinkle

If you . . .

- Want to meet and work with wonderful women
- Like to play and to express yourself
- Want to transform some personal life-issue
- Want to learn and practice various healing 'Sexercises' and 'Super Sex Technologies'
- Want to experience the invigoration of performing live
- Have a desire to see our society mature sexually
- Would like to encourage a fresh, new feminist view of sexuality
- Want to learn more about 'sex magic' as a way to gain access to powerful energy to fuel your wishes and dreams so they come true
- Want to be an 'erotic pioneer' and 'pleasure activist'

. . . Then come along with us on our sensual magical mystery tour.

NO TALENTS OR SKILLS ARE REQUIRED. JUST BE YOURSELF.

Each MetamorphoSex event is unique, tailored to satisfy the individual needs and desires of the women who participate.

Twenty-four women of all ages, races, shapes, sexual preferences, in various phases of their sexual evolution, will gather for several evenings to connect, learn, prepare and create in a workshop format. We will then perform three sex-magic ritual happenings in which a theater audience will be invited to share; to inspire us, co-create with us, and bear witness to our magnificence. (Although this event will likely have some nudity, nudity is not required.)

YOUR SENSUAL MAGICAL MYSTERY TOUR GUIDES will be Annie Sprinkle and Barbara Carrellas. With Linda M. Montano as 'Special Spiritual Consultant.'

The performance/ritual

(Pre-show. THE THEATER OF SENSUAL DELIGHTS – *As audience members enter the theater and wait for the 'main performance' to begin, cast members do some action to stimulate their senses with a Sensorium. Each cast member can choose her own action, and wear whatever costume she wants, but keeps breasts and pubis covered. She brings her own props if needed. For example, she can tickle necks with feathers, feed with chocolates, invite people to smell a gardenia, vibrate shoulders with a vibrator, whisper a poem in people's ears, rub cheeks with a piece of rabbit fur, let people sniff from a bottle filled with a lovely scent, apply glitter to audience members' third eye, massage hands, sit on laps, etc. Or the cast member can choose to hang out in the dressing room with 'the girls' if she's not in the mood to be among the audience.*

When the show is ready to start, the entire cast goes into the dressing room.)

ACT 1. MEET YOUR TOUR GUIDES (Introduction by ANNIE and BARBARA)
(ANNIE and BARBARA enter and go center stage. Cast members are backstage, changing their costumes if they want to. They can opt to include some nudity.)

AS: Hello, I'm Annie Sprinkle.

BC: And I'm Barbara Carrellas.

AS: For the past seven years Barbara Carrellas, Linda Montano and I have been teaching women's Sacred Sex workshops. We found these to be so powerful and entertaining that we wanted to somehow share them with more people. And here we are.

BC: We printed a flyer inviting women to participate. Twenty-six incredible women answered our call. They came from all backgrounds, have various sexual preferences and are all at different phases in their sexual evolutions. We got together every night this week and here are some of the things we did.

AS: First I taught them my basic Sexercise routine: a series of techniques designed to build, move and utilize sexual energy. We did things like kegals, pelvis undulations, ecstasy breathing, the microcosmic orbit, the Chakra Chant, Kundalini meditations and Tantra yoga techniques.

BC: We learned basic sex magic – how you can dedicate your sexual energy and your orgasms to some purpose or goal, like healing an emotional or physical wound, getting a new car, peace in Bosnia, or finding a cure for AIDS. We explored our many sexual personas, especially the big taboo ones, like the witch, bitch, dyke and whore. We discovered the amazing possibilities of energy orgasms. We learned erotic massage strokes like Over Eggs Easy, Pussy Petting, Twist and Shout, and everyone's favorite, Rock Around the Clit Clock. We spent a lot of time learning how to practice safe sex. We learned that safe sex could be mind-blowing sex and discovered that it's so much easier to feel emotionally safe when we are physically safe. Everything you will see in tonight's performance follows strict safe-sex protocol.

We supported each other as we shared stories of our past sexual abuse and pain. We talked about how we have different needs and desires at various times in our lives, and how we can honor and include them all. We talked about how the sexiest thing in the world is simply being in your own truth in the moment.

You will see many of the techniques we learned this week used in various ways on stage tonight. All the women have chosen their own roles. This is their performance.

AS: So now we are ready to put it all together and we want to share it with you. We hope you will enjoy this evening, that it might stimulate some thought and conversation, provoke some feeling, realization, and/or inspiration. Or at least, bring you some pleasure. Let's begin!

ACT 2.   VOICES FROM THE VULVA

(Cast members get into a V-shaped line and chant a special chant while each woman individually takes the 'talking pussy puppet,' steps up to a micro-phone, and says something from her vulva – as if her vulva is speaking. Sug-gested topics: a dedication, a wish, an emotion, a brief story . . . whatever comes to mind, we speak it. This way the audience gets to know us all a bit as individuals.)

ACT 3.   INVOCATION AND CASTING A CIRCLE

(Linda Montano sets the tone and does her magic. About 15 minutes, improvised.)

ACT 4.   ENERGY BUILDING

(The cast prepares the stage: sets up massage tables, lights a flame (in a bowl), puts down things to lay on, and sets the props. Audience members are seated, watching. Each audience member is offered a rattle, and is invited to

shake it when desired. Stage lights are flowing, pulsing, and changing colors, with patterns of light. Then for the next 40 minutes, cast members proceed to build erotic energy. The night before each show, cast members put their names on a sign-up sheet saying what part they will 'perform.' They could choose to do ecstasy breathing, give/receive erotic massage, masturbate, do erotic dance, be a voyeur, be a meditator, shave and powder someone's body, sit in the audience, etc. When the cast chooses what they will do on the night before, they can prepare, and BARBARA and ANNIE can get an idea of what the show might be like, and be sure that it is well balanced. Each cast member has total freedom to do as much, or as little, as she wants to do, or to do nothing at all, thus honoring whatever mood she is in at the time. It's always her choice. About 40 minutes.)

ACT 5.   CLIMAX
(BARBARA CARRELLAS leads everyone in a synchronized Big Draw to climactic music: twenty fast breaths, three deep breaths, holding the third breath for about 20 seconds while clenching the entire body, then we totally let go and relax completely. This creates an energetic climax and an 'ejection of consciousness.')

ACT 6.   BASKING IN THE AFTERGLOW
(Performers 'hold the space,' keeping hands and arms open. Surrendering to whatever feelings are there, or not there. There is no talking. Often there is some laughing, crying, orgasm, intense feelings of bliss . . . this part is often described as 'spiritual.' This section is about 15 to 20 minutes.)

ACT 7.   VOICES FROM THE VULVA – PHASE 2
(ANNIE invites cast and audience to speak out a thought, feeling, realization, make a sound, if they are moved to, Quaker-meeting style. About 5 to 10 minutes.)

ACT 8.   OPEN THE CIRCLE AND GOODBYES
(LINDA MONTANO does some closure, improvised.)

AS: Ladies and Gentlemen, our evening together has COME to an end, literally and figuratively. Please make your way out to our lovely café and enjoy a little food, drink and schmoozing. Please be sure you feel grounded before you get into your car and drive.

BC: We would like to thank the *(name)* theater for having us here. They are very courageous and gracious.

AS and BC: Y'all come back now, ya'here! Good night!

END

Wedding portrait of Annie Sprinkle and Kimberly Silver taken in Provincetown, Massachusetts, in 1995. © Annie Sprinkle and Brad Fowler. Photo: Brad Fowler.

Peace in Bed

Part of my job being in theater has been to do lots of marketing and promotion. Generally I work on my own press releases, and if I'm not way too busy, I get involved in the publicity process to promote an upcoming show. I want as many people to see the show I'm doing as possible. It's a lot more fun to perform for a full house, it pays better, and if people want to know about the show, they can come see it. I've joked that my guardian angels are excellent press agents, because I have been incredibly lucky getting publicity, even when many of my peers couldn't.

For years I made myself available to the media. The arrangement was mutually beneficial. They got some provocative, titillating stories. I got to disseminate my messages: a call to decriminalize and destigmatize sex work, to promote sex-positive attitudes and encourage more and better sex education.

The idea of publicity stunts and media events has always intrigued me, ever since 1969 when I heard about my favorite Beatle, John Lennon, getting married to conceptual artist Yoko Ono, and inviting the press into their honeymoon suite. John and Yoko utilized the enormous media attention their marriage was getting to protest the war in Vietnam. They stayed in bed for one week in an Amsterdam hotel, and again in Montreal. Naturally, the press expected Mr. and Mrs. Lennon to make love, or to at least see them nude. But instead, John and Yoko were wearing white pajamas buttoned up to their necks. *Peace in Bed* was brilliant, and it definitely contributed to ending the war.

When I was on tour in Australia I came up with the *Peace in Bed* concept. I was booked to appear in the prestigious Adelaide Theater Festival. Their publicist was planning a press conference to promote the show, and lots of media had shown interest in attending. I had just gotten married to my girlfriend Kimberly Silver. Our resemblance to John and Yoko was uncanny! I was a misunderstood conceptual artist with long hair and a white button-up nightgown. Kim sang and played guitar, wore John Lennon-style granny glasses and was pretty butch. And we had a message: There is a

Peace in Bed event with Annie Sprinkle, Kimberly Silver and members of the media, in Zurich, Switzerland. Photo: © Niklaus Strauss.

war going on in people's bedrooms – people are ignorant, fearful, and confused about sex, unsatisfied, lying to their spouses, there is rape, abuse, unwanted pregnancy, too much sexually transmitted disease, etc. etc. and we must have better sex education.

On 11 March 1996 we did a two-hour long *Peace in Bed* performance. Originally we were booked to do it at the Hilton Hotel, but when they heard it was a press conference for a 'porn star,' they said no way. We moved to the more slut-positive Hyatt. We made the front page of all the major Australian newspapers and were covered on all the national news programs. Our thirty-show tour completely sold out. We didn't even show our tits.

We did *Peace in Bed* again in Zurich, Hamburg, Montreal and Northampton. (It was a long honeymoon.) We were really excited to have booked the exact same hotel room that John and Yoko used for their Montreal Bed Peace, but the hotel wouldn't allow us to do it when they heard we were two women. The same day that we did *Peace in Bed*, Sinead O'Connor and the Premier of Quebec also had press conferences. We got ten times more and better media coverage than they did. The following day, the Premier of Quebec was quoted in the press as saying, 'I should have been in bed with Annie Sprinkle.'

AHOY! ARTISTS AND SEX WORKERS UNITE!

Annie Sprinkle & Performance Space 122 invite you aboard . . .

The Liberty Love Boat

Columbus Day cruise to the Statue of Liberty to celebrate

Freedom of Creative Sexual Expression

Join us on a Tit-tanic journey to the isle of the Goddess of Freedom.

Our message this day: Let it be known from sea to shining sea that we utilize sexually explicit words, pictures, and performances to communicate our ideas and emotions, and contribute our love to the world. We are decent, caring citizens and we will be free to explore and share our bodies/ourselves. We denounce sexual censorship – including Mayor Giuliani's new zoning laws – as anti-art, ignorant, mean and inhumane.

At the statue we will take turns sharing our statements/ performances/actions/meditations/dances/speeches/prayers/ poems about censorship and freedom. Then, for posterity, our group will pose with the Statue of Liberty for a herstoric photograph by renowned photographer Dona Ann McAdams.

Columbus Day. Monday, October 12 1998

1:30 Gather in Battery Park.

2:00 Take public ferry to the Statue of Liberty ($6).

3:00 Performances and group photo.

4:30 Return to Battery Park, or visit Ellis Island if you wish.

Bring signs, flags, props, propaganda, performances, energy, etc.

Dress as: Magic mermaids, slutty sailors, super-strippers, art pimps, chocolate- and blood-smeared performance artists, erotic fish, sexual healers, scandalous politicians with interns, happy hookers, avant-garde octopussy, kinky conquistadors, or???

Your shipmates will be artists and sex workers, Betty Dodson, Quentin Quisp, Shelly Mars, COYOTE (Sex workers rights organization), Kate Bornstein, Barbara Carrellas, MOSEX, Ducky Doolittle, Caterina Bartha, Dr. Carol Queen and Dr. Robert Lawrence, ISWFACE (International Sex Worker Foundation for Art, Culture and Education), Martha Wilson and Franklin Furnace, Diane Torr, *Porn Free* magazine, Spider Webb, Angel's Home of Burlesque, Toys in Babeland, Erospirit Institute, Jennifer Blowdryer, Hell Fire Club, Alicia Relles, Gates of Heck, Grand Opening's Kim Aires, Don Shewey, Veronica Vera's Academy for Boys Who Want to Be Girls, NY Body Archive, Tristan Taormino, and many others.

Liberty Love Boat

After having not been in Manhattan for a few years, I was returning to do a three-week run of my *Herstory of Porn* show at Performance Space 122. Since I had left the city, several of my good friends in the sex industry had been run out of business by Mayor Giuliani. The sleazy charm of 42nd Street was totally gone. Porn theater and peep-show doors had been padlocked, closed by police. I was worried that maybe my show at P.S. 122 would get shut down. I wanted to see and support my New York City friends, celebrate what was left of our freedom, make a political statement, and I'm always up for a nice boat ride, so I created the *Liberty Love Boat* event, which P.S. 122 helped me to organize.

It had rained for a week straight. The sun came out just in time for our excursion. About 200 artists and sex workers showed up, most of them dressed in 'wild' clothes and costumes. As soon as we arrived we were surrounded by police cars, police boats and police helicopters. They videotaped our every move and really harassed us. It seems that because of the way we were dressed, they assumed we were going to bomb the Statue of Liberty. Although we had a permit to gather and to do a photograph, they said if we held up our signs, they would arrest us. (We would need a different permit for that.) We explained that our signs were photo props not protest signs. That didn't work. We opted not to get arrested and be relatively cooperative.

At the base of the Statue of Liberty, we formed a big circle and I passed around a megaphone. We all took turns doing our performances/speeches/rituals. Tourists from all over the world were either shocked or delighted by our presence and asked if their families could pose for snapshots with us. The Goddess of Freedom smiled down upon us.

Cruising to the Statue of Liberty on the 'Liberty Love Boat' with Annie Sprinkle (wearing mermaid tail), Alicia Kay, Murry Hill, Julia Everding, Carol Queen, Barbara Carrellas, Kari Jewel, and other artists and sex workers. Photo: © Dona Ann McAdams.

'The Group Photo' at the *Liberty Love Boat* event, with police surveillance helicopter. Photo: © Dona Ann McAdams.

Annie Sprinkle in the opening scene of *Herstory of Porn*. © Annie Sprinkle and Leslie Barany. Photo Leslie Barany.

Annie Sprinkle's Herstory of Porn

(Directed by Emilio Cubeiro;
written and performed by Annie Sprinkle)

Although this performance tells the story of my own personal sexual evolution, I have found that people very much relate it to their own life experiences. The show starts with me playing myself when I was eighteen years old, and goes up to the present (me in my mid-forties). I play seven different personas. The story takes place in seven different movie theaters. Each theater has a different (imaginary) projectionist. The seven phases I go through are illustrated with tightly edited sex film clips, from many of the 150 feature films I made over the years. The dialog printed in bold type is delivered when there are no film clips showing. Dialog in regular type is delivered while film clips are showing.

If you happen to know about the Chakra system, it's interesting to note that the seven phases ('Loops') parallel the seven Chakras, from the bottom to the top – artist Linda Montano's influence. Generally my shows are tightly scripted, but I tend to revise scripts as I perform them, and I improvise lines whenever I want to.

The play starts out intentionally raunchy, misogynist and violent, then evolves into a more artistic, spiritual, feminist perspective. I wanted to illustrate the wide variety of types of sexuality, to educate people on the many different genres of pornography, and to let them get to know a 'porn star' in an honest, deeply intimate way. This show examines issues of censorship, sex work, gender, personal growth, sexuality in our culture, self-acceptance, filmmaking, shame, aging, etc.

You can view most of the film clips used in the stage show in the made-for-video version of *Herstory of Porn* which I co-directed with Scarlot Harlot (available from Good Vibrations, San Francisco, www.goodvibes.com). However, the video script is somewhat different from the stage script. In this script, I have edited out dialog that really doesn't make any sense without viewing the film clips simultaneously.

This script evolved out of an earlier version of a film diary show I did called *Hardcore from the Heart* which was directed and dramaturgued by Daniel Banks. I performed it for eight months internationally with my girlfriend at the time, Kimberly Silver, who also worked as my stage manager. Kim made a large contribution to this film diary.

(Preset: The stage is set to look like the stage of a movie theater, with movie screen and movie theater seats. To set a nostalgic, feminine mood, the audience enters to music tape of female jazz vocalists Sarah Vaughan, Billie Holiday, and Dinah Washington playing softly. The lights on stage and in the house are low and sexy. Preset slide image of a sleazy porn movie ticket booth with Annie Sprinkle's name on the marquee.)

(Music off. Blackout.)

Act 1

LOOP 1: The Early Porn

(Stage lights come up. ANNIE is making cartoon-like porno orgasm sounds from back stage. Through the headset microphone she wears throughout the show, the audience can hear her when she's back stage.)

Ohhh, oh that's so good. More. Harder. No, stop! STOP IT! I'VE GOT TO GO ON NOW. STOP!

(ANNIE swaggers to center stage, disheveled, spilling popcorn from a box she's holding, as she enters. ANNIE is in her wide-eyed, eighteen-year-old, naïve bimbo persona, wearing a checkered dress, pigtails and chewing gum.)

Hi. Welcome to the Pink Pussycat Sinema. My name is Annie Sprinkle and I'm a porno starlet! And tonight I'm going to share with you'all my intimate film diary!

Hmmmm, what a sexy audience. We're going to have fun.

You're probably wondering how a nice girl like me got into porno. Well, it all started with popcorn. I was eighteen years old. That was last year, in 1973. And I got a job in a movie theater selling popcorn. They were showing a new movie called *Deep Throat*. I had never seen a porno movie before and after work I went in to watch it, and I was totally shocked ... and excited. The movie only played for a few weeks, and then the police closed the movie theater down and there was a big obscenity trial. I was called as a very

important witness, because I sold the popcorn. It was there in the courtroom that I met the star of **Deep Throat**, Linda Lovelace herself, and the director, Gerard Damiano. I asked Jerry if he would teach me how to deep throat. He did. I became his mistress, followed him to New York City, and the rest is porn HERstory.

Want to see some of my flicks? OK Guido, start the projector!

(START VIDEO)

This is my first movie, *Teenage Deviate*. I'm at the psychiatrist's office. I was eighteen here, but the director wanted me to look younger, so I'm wearing pigtails, chewing gum and playing cards. I play a virgin. We were expected to be good girls and not like sex. Guido, stop, stop!

(STOP VIDEO WITH PAUSE BUTTON as man unzips pants and is about to reveal his penis.)

STOP! Stop! Is everyone here over eighteen? Because what you're gonna see next is very sexually explicit. If for any reason there's something you don't want to watch, just cover your eyes, and it will pass. And please try to keep an open mind until the very end. I want to take you on a long journey. OK, Guido, I think they're ready now.

(START VIDEO)

In porn you always tell the guy his penis is too big no matter what size. Wife swapping is a popular theme. This one is called *Wet Xmas*. We were really just a bunch of hippies having lots of wild sex and orgies anyways. Why not get paid for all that free love? I got $100 for this movie, plus cab fare. *(clip of young ANNIE smoking marijuana)* I smuggled that pot in from Mexico myself.

This one was called the *Streets of Sin Francisco*, filmed entirely in New York. It's an interracial detective thriller! This one is called *Teenage Career Girls*. A lot of girls won't work with black guys, but I think they're so hot! When I got into porn I shaved off all of my pubic hair so the fans could see every juicy detail. It's called the porno cut. See the toothbrush? *(ANNIE putting toothbrush into her vagina)* That was my idea, to use the toothbrush. I brush after every meal. Look ma, a big cavity! I think it's hot when it's raunchy and nasty. Don't you?

This one is called *Teenage Masseuse*. This is my first ever girl-girl scene. I didn't know what I was doing, but she seemed to like it anyways. Most people haven't really had a chance to look at other people's genitals all big and close up, and I think genitals are so beautiful, don't you? This was a really good director. He said 'let his dick fall out and then put it back in.' I thought that was really effective. I was one of the first girls to get a tattoo! I hung the wallpaper in this scene myself.

This is an adult fairy tale. *(ANNIE having sex with a dwarf wearing a frog costume)* That's the famous Marc $10\frac{1}{2}''$ Stevens. That's my friend Helen Madigan. We love working together because we never fake it. Some girls do, you know. You can almost feel that big dick in your mouth. That's the famous Vanessa Del Rio. We play fashion models. We have to sell our new line of lingerie to the all-male buyers, so Vanessa puts lipstick on my pussy lips then licks it off. I thought that was really dumb. But it felt really good!

This film was made by a woman who was about sixty years old, Doris Wishman. All her life she wanted to make horror movies, but couldn't raise the money for her horror movie. Finally she got the money to make a porno movie. When it was all done, her porno movie came out looking a lot like a horror movie. In this scene, this woman's husband dies. He was a very jealous man, and every time she has sex, his ghost comes back to haunt her. The film Alfred HitchCOCK always wanted to make, but never had the guts. People ask me if having sex on camera is embarrassing. That's easy. It's the acting that's embarrassing. I only had one method-acting class. *(ANNIE gets stabbed with a knife by a ghost.)* Right between the breasts!

This director was a big fan of that Swedish director, Ingmar Bergman. He wanted to make a film with more drama and passion and depth, so I get fucked with a big fat kilbassi sausage. That sausage felt really great, and it fed the entire cast and crew for lunch.

Suddenly porn movies became chic, and the budgets got bigger. They started adding production values, and special effects. We started doing films based on famous movies, and TV shows. Can you guess which movie this is a copy of? *(Titles come on reading 'Smash'd.')* I wanted the part of Hot Lips. She had the best sex scenes. But instead I got the part of Gail, a kind nurse who gives her patients blow jobs while they're sleeping.

I got my name in lights on Broadway with this movie, *Kathy's Graduation Present*. Here I do a DP, that's a double penetration.

(close-up of testicles bouncing) Couldn't you just watch those testicles for ever? OK, here comes the money-shot. I tried to get both guys to cum at the same time. The first guy came before the camera started rolling. It happens. But not with Jamie Gilles. Jamie was such a professional, he could count down from ten to his orgasm.

I've prepared a little cum-shot medley for you. Coming attractions! Get it? Here I play a nurse who must collect sperm samples in little jars.

(STOP VIDEO. Lights come up.)

LOOP 2: Kinky Porn

(ANNIE transitions into a dominatrix persona, wearing a fetish maid costume and spiked high heels.)

You know, making straight sex movies is nice, but I'm the kind of girl who likes to experiment. So, at a certain point I started exploring different kinds of fetishes and fantasies. Nothing that I, or anyone else, could dream up seemed too bizarre or kinky or taboo. I wanted to try everything with everyone. The more conservative porn directors wouldn't hire me any more. They said I was 'too kinky.' Oh well, you can't please everybody.

Wanna see some of my kinky movies? *(Some audience members applaud.)* **I could tell you were a very kinky audience. We'll have to go to a special theater, to the Hell Hole Room in the basement of the Mitchell Brother's theater in SIN Francisco where they show the really kinky stuff. OK, Jim and Artie, start the projector! Now!**

(START VIDEO)

Leather and whips and chains, oh my! When I got to the set that morning they said, 'Annie, we're going to put you in bondage.' I'd never even heard of such a thing. In principle I didn't really want to make violent porn movies, but I remember I really needed the money at that time. And they were paying $500 a day. Plus I wanted to try everything. The director of this film, Phil Prince, went to jail for life for killing his business partner and his wife. He seemed like such a nice guy.

Here I was kidnapped and raped and forced to fist-fuck one of the other prisoners. That's Crisco. It makes THE best lube for fisting. Billy could take anything up his butt. His favorite was a whole rack of billiard balls. You put 'em in and he shoots 'em out. Want to see that part? *(Screen flashes the word CENSORED across it.)* CENSORED!!! I hate that. *(First Amendment text appears on screen.)* Ah, saved by the First Amendment. I love our country. *(ANNIE bends over, ass to audience, and pulls the American flag from a hole in her panties. Then waves the flag proudly.)* We have so much freedom here, but they keep trying to take it away. We have to keep on fighting for it over and over.

Let's pick up with a little hot amputee action! I was never shy about my bodily fluids, my smells or tastes. In fact, I enjoyed them. This is the first piercing scene ever in a porno movie. *(graphic labia-piercing scene)* Oh, it really doesn't hurt much. It's just like piercing a potato chip. *(foot-licking scene)* I put my heart and SOLE into this one. Good FOOTAGE!

This is a science fiction porn movie directed by Gerard Damiano himself. That's my real-life lover, Mal O'Ree. Casual sex is nice, but when you're in love, it's something extra special. My favorite thing in the world is doing analingus.

Of all of my cum-shots, this one is my best one. I think it's the music. Slow motion works so well for cum-shots. And it's shot in 35 millimeter. *(Annie slapping a penis)* Penis torture movies are so popular. They sold thousands of these for $89.95. The guys just eat 'em up. Here we are, The Sisters of Perpetual Punishment doing religious practices at the convent. *(golden shower scene)* They don't call me Sprinkle for nothin'. I like sex all wet and gushy and slippery.

This film is about a cult of devil worshipers. When I did this movie I was having a lot of erotic fantasies about being raped. *(intense scene where ANNIE is raped by five 'devil worshipers')* So I decided to act it out, and the scene got rougher than I had anticipated. I got a bit bruised up, and almost really got hurt. I got kind of scared. That's when I realized that just because something really turns you on it doesn't necessarily mean it's good for you. After that I never had any more rape fantasies.

(STOP VIDEO. Lights up.)

LOOP 3: Deep inside Annie Sprinkle – Movie Theater Scene, and Masturbation Scene

(ANNIE transitions into a sultry empowered porn-star persona, now an

accomplished seductress. She is wearing a tight, sequined Hollywood movie queen sheath dress.)

After making about a hundred porn movies, written, produced and directed all by men, I felt like I wanted to make something of my own. Something from a woman's point of view. So I sat down at my typewriter and wrote up a six-page script. I found a guy with lots of money, gave him the best blow job I knew how, and he agreed to produce my movie. It was called ***Deep inside Annie Sprinkle.*** And it became the number two biggest-grossing porn film in 1982 . . . and the beginning of a new era, pornography made by women. Let's go to Times Square in NYC to the Orleans Theater. OK Tyrone, start my film.

(START VIDEO. This film scene is from Deep inside Annie Sprinkle, *where ANNIE goes into a movie theater and has sex with porn fans in the audience.)*

I wanted to make something in which the viewers were not just sitting watching, but more involved. Something more intimate. So throughout the film I talk directly into the camera. This scene was filmed at a time when there were over a thousand porno movie theaters all across the United States.

(As video shows street in NYC where the Orleans Theater is located, ANNIE slowly and sexily walks (mimicking her walk in the video) across stage to where a cardboard standee of ANNIE in a corset is set up with a black feather boa around its shoulders. ANNIE is wearing the same dress that she is seen wearing in the film. ANNIE mimics the on-screen dialog.)

You know, I am a real exhibitionist and I love to have sex in very public places. Sometimes, if I see one of my movies is playing, I'll go in and sit down and start watching myself fucking and sucking on that big screen, and that makes me very, very horny. So I get carried away and I start doing all the guys around me. It's really nice. So don't be surprised if you're ever in a movie theater and I come in and I sit right next to you.

(ANNIE picks up a vibrator, walks out into the audience, and plays around with the audience, sitting on laps, putting her boobs in faces, teasing, which is also what is happening in the movie on screen.)

Now I became the aggressor. No one had to force ME into sex. I was the one who wanted it, and the men just better watch out.

(improvisation) Who wants to play? Massage? Isn't this just like in the movies? What's that big wet spot? Did you cum already? Are you lesbians? You can touch me anywhere you want to . . .

(When masturbation scene starts on the movie screen, ANNIE walks back on to stage and puts vibrator onto her projected on-screen pussy.)

When I made this movie, a lot of people, including many porn directors, weren't sure if women could actually have real orgasms. And even if they could, they weren't important anyways, because there was no sperm! But now I was directing. I wanted to show a real woman's orgasm. Luckily we had plenty of film in the camera. *(ANNIE interacts with her own movie image of herself masturbating.)* I know you love it, come on baby. YES! I LOVE YOU. THAT'S RIGHT. YES! Oh, you're coming again . . .

(Movie image changes to ANNIE in a park talking into the camera. ANNIE mimics screen dialog.)

I have had such a wonderful, horny time with you. *(kiss)* I love you. You know, even with all that sex I've been having, I still feel kind of horny. I hope we run into each other very, very soon.

(Spotlight, mirror ball, disco lights. ANNIE blows kiss and struts like a showgirl to front of stage dragging feather boa. ANNIE goes behind curtain, throws boa out onto stage. Spotlight stays on until ANNIE's boa falls to floor. As video ends and lights come up – slowly.)

Intermission

(Slide of an upscale movie theater ticket booth comes up. Music is played, which is more modern and New Age-y.)

Act 2

LOOP 4: Rites of Passion

(Lights fade to black. Center stage lights come up. ANNIE is in her New Age Girl persona, dressed in rainbow-colored, flowing Goddess gown.)

(ANNIE from off-stage) **OOOMMMMMMMMMMM ... Nam**

Annie Sprinkle masturbating herself masturbating in the film *Deep Inside Annie Sprinkle*, during *Herstory of Porn*. Photo: © Dona Ann McAdams.

ma she vaya. Oommm. *(ANNIE enters, still clinging to the final MMMMMMMMMM.)*

(ANNIE center stage) **MMMMM. Namaste. Welcome to Taos, New Mexico, to the New Age Sex Multiplex. Did you try some of that delicious organic popcorn? It's so good for you. Did you have enough time to process the first half? It took ME several years. Are you ready to continue the porn film herstory?** *(Audience says 'yes.')*

Whenever I discovered some new sexual experience I'd become extremely enthusiastic and I'd want to share my experience with the whooole planet. And that's just what happened the time I met a very magical, erotically gifted man named Jamel. He had just come back from India where he was practicing ancient Tantric sexual yoga techniques. I got to spend three incredible days and nights in bed with him making love, and he taught me some incredible things. And it was the first time I had a truly spiritual experience – through sex. I wanted to share with people what it felt like, so I wrote, directed and edited *Rites of Passion*. Ma Prem Mahamudura, please enlighten us.

(START VIDEO)

This video was produced by my good friend Candida Royalle. She wanted to make 'erotica for couples.' The porn industry said it would never sell, but it did very well.

Although this was my autobiographical story I hired a beautiful, young, blonde actress to play me: Jeanna Fine. The film starts with the young woman, me, becoming increasingly dissatisfied with the kind of sex she had been having. It all seemed so mechanical, so genitally focused. She wasn't feeling connected with her lovers. She knew there had to be more to it than that. Then she meets her spirit guide who teaches her ancient sexual secrets.

(Erotic footage of cosmic love-making scene with lots of psychedelic special effects. ANNIE is acting very New Age-y.)

I wanted to do a scene that was more sensuous, where the sex was slower and more meditative. Where it wasn't all so genitally focused but more full-bodied. Where the lovers connect with their hearts, and eyes.

When you are making love, do you ever feel like you don't know where you start, and your lover begins, and you're melting

Annie Sprinkle in her 'New Age Girl' persona during *Annie Sprinkle's Herstory of Porn*. Photo: © Dona Ann McAdams.

into each other? You become one with the Universe? Do you ever feel like you're in your body, yet you're out of your body, like you're floating in space? You become pure energy, vibration . . .

I decided not to go for the standard cum-shot on the face, but to try to create a cosmic orgasm of love, so I borrowed a special effect from *Star Trek*.

(ANNIE in a lotus position, prayerfully recites live the same words heard on screen.)

> IT IS TIME WE REMEMBER SEX
>   AS BEING THE TRULY SACRED ACT THAT IT IS.
> A DEEP MEDITATION,
>   A DANCE OF THE FORCES OF CREATION.

(STOP VIDEO)

LOOP 4/Continued: Safer-Sex Video

It's a good thing that when I made that movie it was all shot softcore. There was no actual penetration. Because shortly after the film was finished, Roger, that healthy-looking body-builder, got horribly sick, and died of AIDS. And some of the people you saw in earlier film clips also died. AIDS spread like wildfire. In my world it was devastating, as I'm sure it was in yours.

I thought about getting out of pornography, of course. But at the same time, I desperately wanted to do something to try to help stop more death from spreading. So I started a group called Pornographers Promoting Safer Sex. I called on the porn industry to help educate the public. I figured if everyone in porn started using safer sex, people could see exactly how to do it and see that safer sex could be hot sex. I thought it could have a huge impact and save lives. Unfortunately the heterosexual porn industry didn't take the challenge to use safe sex, and continued to use almost all unsafe sex. That's when I realized that for the most part, the porn industry wasn't a community that cared about people, but a business that really only cared about money. I was very disappointed.

From then on all my sex films used only safer sex. And the good news was that health education professionals started producing pornography to get their important message

across. Here's an herstorical clip from one of the world's first lesbian safer-sex videos produced by the Gay Men's Health Crisis. Mahamudra, the healing video please.

(START VIDEO)

(lesbian sex scene with ANNIE and a woman using all safe sex)

At first no one really knew exactly what safe sex was, and we had to invent it. This is my first time trying a dental dam. She was my UPS woman.

(STOP VIDEO)

LOOP 5: Art Porn

(ANNIE wears a black velvet dress with Mona Lisa painted across her chest, and a black artist's beret.)

Eventually, making mainstream commercial pornography was no longer what I wanted to do with my life. I had a deep, dark, secret fantasy. What I really wanted was to be an artist. *(ANNIE puts on a pretentious artist persona.)* **So I started appearing in films that were more 'arty,' more conceptual, experimental, avant-garde, political, feministic, educational, and not simply focused on being erotic. Films made by artists.**

Let's go to the Museum of Modern Art and see some art porn. Oh, I am sorry you can't eat any popcorn during this part. The museum is NEA funded, and food is not allowed. *(tinge of bitchy)* **OK Curator, have your intern start the deck!**

(START VIDEO)

WAR IS MENSTRUAL ENVY – This is a film by Nick Zedd, who is kind of like the James Dean of the experimental film world. I'm not sure what this scene has to do with war or menstrual envy, but that's what I love about art. It doesn't have to make sense. You have total creative freedom. And there's a lot less censorship in art than in porn. That's a very talented performance artist named Kembra Pfahler, from the East Village, who has a really cool band called Karen Black Band. This film won several prestigious awards.

BUBBLES GALORE – This is a film by a young Canadian artist, named Cynthia Roberts, who did some very clever casting. *(Screen*

Annie Sprinkle in her 'Artist' persona during *Annie Sprinkle's Herstory of Porn*. Photo: © Dona Ann McAdams.

reads title 'Annie Sprinkle as God.') Whenever I, God, get turned on, it inspires the women down on earth to make pornography.

Do you know the difference between erotica and pornography? In erotica you just use a feather, in porn you use the whole chicken. Or as my friend Gloria Leonard jests, 'it's all in the lighting.'

LINDA/LES & ANNIE – THE FIRST FEMALE-TO-MALE TRANSSEXUAL LOVE STORY – Just when you think you've done it all, something new comes along! This video is the true story about the night my female-to-male transsexual lover and I tried out his brand-new surgically constructed penis for the very first time. I created a new film genre I coined 'docu-porn.' It was a big hit on the gay and lesbian film festival circuit.

(STOP VIDEO)

Eventually I wanted to make my own art film. So I put all my time, energy, and money into my own project. I didn't care if anyone liked it, or if it made any money. I just did it my way. Well, it went on to play in some very important film festivals, art galleries, and museums. I created yet another new film genre I coined 'Post-Porn Modernism.'

The truth was I had become ... a lesbian. But no one would believe that *I* was a lesbian. I was having trouble meeting women. So I made this film to help gain access into the lesbian world. And it worked! Let's go to the screening of THE SLUTS AND GODDESSES VIDEO WORKSHOP OR HOW TO BE A SEX GODDESS IN 101 EASY STEPS. Curator, please!

(START VIDEO)

THE SLUTS AND GODDESSES VIDEO WORKSHOP

(This video clip has a lot of voiceovers, so there's not much talking live. I pace on the stage as if I'm a very arrogant film-maker.)

I applied for NEA grants for this film but didn't get them. You see so many sex films and videos, and you never see the afterglow. To me that is the most precious and delicious part of lovemaking. So here I filmed a long afterglow scene.

(STOP VIDEO)

LOOP 6: Masturbation Memoirs

(ANNIE as her present self, a mature woman persona, wearing plain, brown, earth mother-style clothes)

Sometimes I wonder if maybe I'm getting too old to be making porno movies? I'm forty-three now, and my body is really changing. Everything is bigger and softer and hanging more. I have wrinkles.

But personally, I find other older women really sexy. Even more sexy than younger women. There's a ripeness, a depth, a power, an awesome sensitivity and awareness. There's all that knowledge and experience. I think older women are the new sex symbols. We just have to make a new kind of porn that reflects who we are and what we like.

A year ago, I decided to make a video that celebrated my maturity. Plus I also had moved to the country and I was inspired by the incredible eroticism of being out in nature. It's called *Masturbation Memoirs*, and it's dedicated to our ex-Surgeon General, Jocelyn Elders.

Let me take you to Northampton, Massachusetts, to the Sappho Film Co-op, and let's see some 'women's self-help porn.' Kimberly, my sweetheart ... That's my wife up there in the booth. We've been together for three years, totally monogamous ... That's largely why this is a masturbation tape. Hon, start the tape!

(START VIDEO)

(film of ANNIE nude, wearing only a crown of flowers, masturbating at the foot of a waterfall)

This video was produced by the House o' Chicks and was filmed in the California redwoods entirely in Vulvascope with the Vulva-cam. Here I am forty-three years old. No corset, no garter belt, no false eyelashes. Just 'au naturel.' This is about how I 'medibate,' which is to masturbate and meditate at the same time. *(ANNIE kisses a tree.)* I came out as a dendraphiliac. Trees are so sexy. I did something really outrageous for this film, I grew out all of my body hair for the first time – and there was a lot of it.

I've talked with so many women who tell me that sometimes when they have an orgasm, they like to have a little cry at the same time. It feels so good, and yet I've never seen it in a film. So I decided to share my crygasm with my sisters. This is a female ejaculation scene. It's the latest feminist craze – women ejaculate and men don't.

(STOP VIDEO)

LOOP 7: Teenage Mermaid Fantasea

(ANNIE is wearing an elegant, floor-length evening gown with ostrich-feather trim. The dress is made of opalescent sequins which sparkle in the light, for the grand finale. The costume says 'Annie Sprinkle has finally arrived, and she's fabulous!')

It's funny, the more I learn about sexuality, the more I realize how much more there is to learn. It's so vast, multi-faceted, and so full of contradictions. It's simply the most interesting subject in the world. Why anyone would want to make a movie about anything else, I don't know.

That brings my story up to the present. It's very strange looking back at those old movies from twenty-five years ago. I had never watched them before and when I saw them I had very mixed feelings. On the one hand, they seem so silly, immature, very unerotic, and some are outright violent, and in retrospect, very misogynist. And on the other hand, some were very creative, and funny, they were baby steps and there's a wonderfully uninhibited quality about them. I came to accept that that was where I was at twenty-five years ago, and that's where a lot of our society was at. We had to start somewhere. One thing is for sure: we have COME a long way. And we're still coming! And there's still a long way to go.

Pornography is like a mirror through which we can take a look at ourselves. And sometimes what we see doesn't look pretty, and it can make us feel VERY uncomfortable. But how beautiful to take that look, to see (truth), and to learn.

THE ANSWER TO BAD PORN IS NOT NO PORN, BUT TO MAKE BETTER PORN!

How many of you here tonight have been involved in pornography in one way or another? Behind the cameras, or in front? Polaroids at home count. Come on, porno pride! Raise those hands high. And how many of you would like to make some kind of porn or erotica? What would you like to

do? *(Hands go up, and audience members share their answers out loud.)* **Great.**

I'd like to show you one last movie. I just finished a little training film to help you get started. OK _____ *(name of actual real-life tech person in booth)* **start the training video please.**

(START TAPE)

(This video was made especially for the end of this show, and was created to interact with live.)

PORNOGRAPHY MADE EASY – First decide if you want to be the director of your movie, the star of your movie, or both. You'll need some kind of camera, plenty of film or videotape, and someone with a good eye. Lights are extremely important. Find the best light person you can, preferably someone really pretty with big muscles. Have a good production manager to keep things moving along. Try not to use your own money, but find some nice producers. Then get on the phone and call up some friends you'd like to have sex with and invite them to be in your movie. You'll need some kind of erotic theme for your movie. Any ideas? *(Audience yells out their ideas, i.e.: 'The President and the Intern! Pizza Delivery Girls! Police Officers in the Castro! Bob Dole on Viagra!')*

TEENAGE MERMAID FANTASEA

(Film of colorful, Disney-esque underwater fantasy scene. ANNIE and a young woman are wearing extravagant mermaid costumes.)

I'd like to make a movie about mermaids. It would be the story of an elder mermaid who initiates a teenage mermaid into the treasures of her sexuality. I'd play the elder mermaid, of course. It wouldn't be like those horrible old Teenage movies I used to make where the teenager was manipulated into the sex. I'd let the young mermaid make all the first moves. Hmmm, there's the first kiss. *(The video cuts back and forth between the sex scene and the behind-the-scenes filming the sex scene.)* You can really mess your lipstick up, so have a make-up artist on the set to keep you looking glamorous. I want lots of ECUs on the erogenous zones.

This is Alicia. I met her when I gave a visiting artist lecture at the University of Santa Cruz. She had learned about me in her Women's Studies course. She wanted to apprentice with me, so I put her in my porn movie. Be sure all your models are over eighteen and get a photocopy of their ID. And be sure you get a signed model release.

You can be in the middle of a sex scene, just about to come, and suddenly your wig falls off. You have to stop everything and fix it, because you're making a movie! Don't think of it as coitus interruptus, but as the creative process.

So the young mermaid has her very first orgasm, and it's a whale of an orgasm! I've got an idea! I could teach the young mermaid how to seduce a diver. A man could arise from the depths. But I haven't had sex with a genetic man in seven years. I forgot how. What will some of my lesbian friends say? They'll be shocked. Well, it is for art . . . Can porn be art? Can art be porn? Art porn, porn art? Who cares what it's called? I just like making it. I want the camera to see his throbbing erection. Why hide it? Mermaids would use green condoms, don't you think? *(Bubble machine starts live bubbles on stage.)* I want lots of tail action!

You know how movies have acting coaches, and voice coaches? It's good to have a sex coach on the set to keep their eye on the sex. Good thing Joe Kramer was there as our sex coach. He pointed out that our dildo was on upside down. *(The diver stud takes a dildo out of his swim-suit.)* Ah, the ecstasy of modern technology! I love the way Raul moves his butt in this part. I could watch it over and over again.

To draw forth concepts from the void, and make them manifest, it's the dance of the forces of creation. I always wanted a fish tail. You can be whoever you want with movie magic. I want a cum-shot. I like them. You can use condensed milk for sperm. It tastes sweet when you lick it all up.

What a thrill having worked a sixteen-hour day, your friends all around you, supporting you, the film is in the can, and soon you'll lovingly begin the editing process, the packaging, the promotion . . .

Then, the diver swims away, and I, having lived a full, pleasure-filled, ecstatic mermaid life, know that soon I'm going to die. So I pass on the torch to the young teenage mermaid, so that she can carry on the tradition, and evolve it in her own way. Then I die a very orgasmic death.

(As on-screen ANNIE *dies, live on-stage* ANNIE *lights a candle. The song 'Teach Me Tonight' by Dinah Washington plays loudly. This is the only music used in the entire show. Movie screen shows one minute of slow-motion*

clips, flashing back through time, through snips of the film clips the audience saw in the show, until we end at the first film clip of the show.)

(STOP TAPE. Blackout. A moment of silence in full blackout. We see and hear ANNIE blow out the candle.)

(Lights come up.)

(After applause, ANNIE invites audience to hang out if interested.)

Thanks for coming. There aren't many theaters in the world where I can go and do this show, so thanks to everyone here at the _____ (theater) for their hospitality.

I'm going backstage to change clothes. I'll be out in a few minutes. Stick around if you'd like to share any of your thoughts or feelings. I'd love to meet you. Good night.

(House lights up softly.)

END

Commentary: *Annie Sprinkle from Reel to Real*

Herstory starts with a kind of faked, muffled cry, the 'obligatory' female orgasm of porn flicks, which, in effect, functions as Annie's mock entrance, and sets the deconstructive tone of the piece. As Williams explains:

> Hard core desires assurance that it's witnessing not the voluntary performance of feminine pleasure, but its involuntary confession. The woman's ability to fake the orgasm that the man can never fake (at least according to certain standards of evidence) seems to be at the root of all the genre's attempts to solicit what it can never be sure of: the out-of-control confession of pleasure, a hard-core frenzy of the visible.
>
> The animating male fantasy of hard-core cinema might therefore be described as the (impossible) attempt to capture visually this frenzy of the visible in a female body whose orgasmic excitement can never be objectively measured.[1]

The brilliance of Annie's send-up is that she remains off stage during this act. When she does appear, she is dressed as herself, in the days when she sold popcorn, during her pre-Damiano, pre-porn industry initiation. Her bimbo-slut, air-head ethos is matched by a pointedly 'innocent' costume, a high-camp replica of Dorothy in the *Wizard of Oz*. In studied Baby-Doll speak, Annie asks us to maintain an open mind until the end of the show, and warns us that some of the images we are about to see might be disturbing. She then gingerly asks the projectionist to start the reel, only to interrupt *Teenage Masseuse* to ask if everyone is over eighteen. From this point on, one clip follows another in a kind of narrative flow of ejaculating penises and secreting pussies as Annie coyly comments on the tricks of the trade. We rapidly learn about the technical jargon of hardcore cinematography: ECU for 'extreme close-up,' DP for 'double penetration, 'porno-cut,' for shaved pubic hair. But Annie's crash course on the predictability of porno-dramaturgy is always somewhat tongue in cheek, a kind of endless pun on cum. But it is also structured as a series of performative speech acts that will effect transformation. As Marla Carlson describes it:

> The story is neither nuanced nor probable, but it mirrors the narrative structure of Sprinkle's early porn films. In the brief excerpts we see, the innocent schoolgirl is repeatedly taken unawares, rapidly seduced and then extensively fucked. There is no particular reason to believe that Sprinkle is telling a life story any more authentic or less pornographic than the films she shows.[2]

Flicks such as *Kneel before Me* and *Night of Submission* inaugurate a costume change. Annie now wears black vinyl gloves and turns herself into a kinky French maid. But she is ambivalent about her experience in S/M bondage and rape fantasies: 'just because something turns you on doesn't mean it's good for you.' She talks about the dangers of crossing consensual lines and mentions the lesions she received after shooting the gang-rape scene in *The Devil Inside Her*. Interestingly, Carlson refers to this moment as a loss of ironic distance, and speaks of Annie's 'performative regret,'[3] the paradoxical position of being caught between a sex-positive ideology and her desire to reject male-dominated pornography.[4]

Though Annie may be 'performing' regret and no longer buying into her role as facilitator of male-identified porn, the more salient turning point of her narrative occurs during her metamorphosis from the bimbo-object of her starlet years ('the sex was easy, acting was the hard part'[5]) to the speaking subject of *Deep Inside Annie Sprinkle*. Here Annie reclaims the agency of her own body, labor and gaze. After changing into the green sequined dress and fur coat that she wears on screen, Annie proudly informs us that she did the blow job (for the producer) free, but got paid $10,000 to be in the film. Her on-screen persona is confident, sexy, empowered. Annie on stage lip-syncs to her image on screen, looking wickedly into the camera: 'I'm glad you came to see me, I want us to become very intimate.' Obviously, the direct address of her first 'auteur' film gives Annie the agency she lacked previously. But on stage, her lip-syncing functions as subversive counter-mimicry, the comical dismantling of previous porno performances.

As the young Annie of *Deep Inside* makes her way from one crotch to another in the darkened auditorium – while the raincoat brigade watches her 'perform' on the large screen – the Annie in

P.S. 122, dressed as herself in the film, starts to work the audience. She walks up and down the aisles, a vibrator in hand, and sits on laps; she invites people to touch her, and offers to massage them. The exchange is as awkward and tense as it is funny. But then, as if to suggest that we have either turned her on, or failed to do so, Annie concludes this section by walking up to the large on-screen image of her open legs, and vibrates her double. Annie at this moment seems to work with Baudrillardian awareness of what truly constitutes obscenity today: the institutionalized confusion of exterior and interior, private and public, the penetration of any space, the end of metaphor.[6] One of her most sexually marked body parts becomes pure imago, an infinitely readable surface of continually available information and pleasure. Somehow, her gesture comes across as a triumph rather than a provocation, the antithesis of the traditionally obscene. As Craig Owens puts it:

> Today there is a whole pornography of information and communication . . . It is no longer the traditional obscenity of what is hidden, repressed, forbidden or obscene; on the contrary, it is the obscenity of the visible, of the all-too-visible, of the more-than-the-visible. It is the obscenity of what no longer has any secret, of what dissolves completely in information and communication. . . . Obscenity begins precisely when there is no more spectacle, no more [private] scene, when all becomes transparence and immediate visibility, when everything is exposed to the harshest and inexorable light of information and communication. [This is] the obscene [that] does away with every mirror, every look, every image. The obscene puts an end to representation. . . .[7]

After the intermission, Annie returns as New Age guru with flowing red hair and a long bohemian dress. Sex is now sacred. In keeping with this deliberately clichéd Eastern appropriation, a sitar can be heard in the background as we are shown clips from *Rites of Passion*, a holistic porn film *in which Annie no longer performs*. Annie's surrogate is a young blonde woman bored with traditional heterosex who embarks on an intergalactic journey in search of more satisfying sex. Annie, still tongue in cheek, but considerably more emotional, speaks of an eroticism of mutual gazes and Tantric sex. She talks about the important move away from working with body fluids in the wake of the AIDS epidemic, and the fact that the mainstream porn industry of the 1980s has continued to put people at risk.

But sentiment and sacredness have seemingly outed the artist. Annie now wears black velvet. The *Mona Lisa* printed on her dress, a French beret on her head, Annie becomes Paloma Picasso, the 'art expert'. She pointedly asks the curator to have the *intern* start the projector. Annie/Paloma lectures on her films *Sluts and Goddesses* as well as *Linda/Les & Annie – the First Female-to-Male Transsexual Love Story* – and, in particular, their picaresque adventures on the night Les and Annie tried out his new surgically constructed penis for the first time.

The clip of *Masturbation Memoirs*, ostensibly screened at the Sappho Film Co-op, might well usher the transformative moment of Annie's performative memoir. Annie on stage watches the now heavier, older Annie on screen speak of the inner beauty and wisdom of older women and demonstrate 'medibation,' a form of meditative masturbation, and a 'crygasm,' in the midst of a forest. As she puts it, 'I went through a lesbian separatist phase, then eventually moved from a place of judgment to a place of compassion and acceptance.'[8] But back at P.S. 122, her last incarnation of herself on screen, in *Teenage Mermaid Fantasea* (which is projected in the present), is utterly surreal. First, Annie asks the audience if they have ever made pornography. A few timid voices respond. She then suggests that she will help inspire the making of good porn by showing us her next film. Annie appears underwater in a giant fish tank as a glamorous but aging mermaid, who is seduced by a younger female denizen of the deep. Reflecting on her impending death (which she hopes will be orgasmic), she passes on the torch of sexual healing and pleasure and porn-making to her erotic devotee, a young mermaid/porn starlet. Once again, Annie explodes the Euclidean dramaturgy of conventional porn. Annie teaches the young mermaid how to seduce divers. But when the young beauty is on the verge of orgasm, the scene is abruptly interrupted in order for her wig to be readjusted; similarly, just as the handsome diver is about to ejaculate, a technician approaches him and adjusts his dildo. Meanwhile, Annie gives advice on how to produce a beautiful cum-shot with condensed milk.

Teenage Mermaid Fantasea is an intimate ritual of self-discovery and leave-taking through the young mermaid's initiation:

> Because I pass the torch at the end, we have a real bond. I hadn't done a movie in several years and had gained weight and it was a big deal. We didn't use Alicia's (the young mermaid) pussy

because I didn't want to drag Alicia into hardcore. I was protecting her somehow.... This could be the last sex film I'll ever make. It's about how, at the end of most everything, we die.... Part of the mermaid project was about accepting men back into my life somehow. I still have hope that there are some good guys. I had sex with thousands of men and then hadn't had sex with any men for seven years. So I needed to get over that self-created taboo too. The end of the film is partly about my father dying. I produced the video with the money he left me.[9]

During the conclusion of *Herstory*, Annie speaks about the aging process, her complicated relationship to an older, fuller body. Performative nostalgia? Perhaps. But she is never a victim. Annie's last gesture on stage is as politically transgressive as it is corny. Dinah Washington sings 'Teach Me Tonight,' while Annie dons angel wings and leaves the stage.

Notes

1. Linda Williams, *Hard Core: Power, Pleasure, and the 'Frenzy of the Visible'* (Berkeley: University of California Press, 1999), p. 50.
2. Marla Carlson, 'Performative pornography: Annie Sprinkle reads her movies,' *Text and Performance Quarterly*, 19 (July 1999), p. 240.
3. *Ibid.*
4. *Ibid.*, p. 241.
5. *Annie Sprinkle's Herstory of Porn – Reel to Real.*
6. Craig Owens, 'The discourse of others: feminists and postmodernism,' in *The Anti-Aesthetic: Essays on Postmodern Culture* (Port Townsend, WA: Bay Press, 1983), p. 130.
7. *Ibid.*, pp. 130–1.
8. Annie Sprinkle, interview with the author, Poughkeepsie, New York, April 2000.
9. *Ibid.*

Part II

Pornographos:
Writings of a Prostitute

My Brushes and Crushes with the Law

California Lawyer magazine invited me to write an article for them. I was delighted to reach a new audience, and to get to tell war stories of my legal battles, both in my sex work and my performance art work. Also, I was dating a lawyer at the time and I wanted to impress her. I wrote this piece during the heat of the O.J. Simpson trial.

My first brush with the law was when I was an eighteen-year-old hippie in Tucson, Arizona. I got a job selling popcorn at a theater that was showing a new movie called *Deep Throat*. The XXX-rated movie was immensely popular: college students, married couples, and all kinds of folk lined up alongside the raincoat brigade to buy their tickets. After several prosperous months, the theater where I worked was shut down and the film confiscated by police. An obscenity trial ensued. I was subpoenaed as a witness for the prosecution and was ordered to hang out in the witness room for two weeks with Linda Lovelace and the film's director Gerard Damiano (a handsome and charming 46-year-old Italian gentleman). Waiting around to be called to the stand was a bit dull, so to pass the time, Damiano gave me 'deep throat lessons.' I had to take the stand briefly, which I consider my first public performance. Fortunately, lawyer Louis Nizer won this important case for freedom of expression, and Damiano and I won each other's hearts.

I moved to New York City to be Gerard's mistress and got a job as an apprentice in film-making at Kirt Films, a company which created dozens of 16mm porn films. The apprenticeship didn't pay anything, so I worked weekends at Spartacus Spa, which in the late 1970s was Manhattan's fanciest 'massage parlor' (legal jargon for whorehouse). I entertained and had sex with all kinds of men, from the rich and famous, to Hassidic Jewish businessmen, from Mafia gangsters, to police officers. Naturally I had quite a few clients who worked as judges and lawyers. The men of the legal profession were generally respectful, good tippers (often we made about the same hourly wage), and always in a hurry to get back to work. They came to me racked with stress and tension, and left feeling relaxed and blissful. I could take pride in my work. I'm convinced that without prostitution, the legal system could not function.

Being that prostitution was/is illegal, it was reassuring to know I always had a lawyer to defend me if need be. Often there were busts and arrests, but lucky for me they always came down on my days off. I continued to do prostitution for twenty years. I've always been involved in the grass-roots movement to decriminalize prostitution – the political cause which is most near and dear to my heart. We've made some baby steps. It's really about time that someone, somehow, challenged the prostitution laws and got them thrown in the garbage where they belong. It is absurd and mean-spirited to make consensual sex a crime.

After several months of working behind the cameras at Kirt Films, I decided it looked like more fun to be in front, so someone wrote me a two-page script called *Teenage Deviate*. After the eighteen hours it took to complete the shooting of this not-so-major motion picture, a porn star was born. I went on to make 150 features and fifty 8mm loops, and have my name in lights on Broadway. Sometimes my films got into legal conflicts. Mostly the film's distributors and producers dealt with these problems, which was great, but I did pay a price. My biggest hit was *Deep inside Annie Sprinkle* (the number two biggest-selling video in 1982), which I not only starred in, but wrote and directed. The producers and distributors decided to self-censor the film because theaters where the film was shown (mostly the Pussycat chain in California) were taking a lot of heat (no pun intended). I was disappointed with the final censored version of my movie, which became known as 'the California version.'

For a couple years I did a stint as a stripper. Traveling the bumpy burlesque trail I got to see just how ridiculous laws could be, and how clever the lawyers could be in helping us get around those laws. For example, in one city the law demanded 'no full nudity.' So we simply kept our g-strings on when we took our bras off, and put our bras back on before we took off our g-strings. It was full nudity, but not all at once. In another city, the law said 'no nudity and liquor allowed at the same address,' so a glass wall was built between the bar and the stage, and each side of the glass was given a different address. In yet another city, the law insisted that 'dancer's nipples had to be covered.' So dancers had to paint them over with clear liquid latex which kept us legal, but made our nipples painfully irritated. Doesn't anyone see how silly this all is? Why do 'citizens have to be protected' from dancing nude women?

Miraculously the only time I was ever actually arrested was in Jamestown, Rhode Island. I was at the home of my friends, erotic entrepreneurs Mickey and Susan Leblovic and Dutch artist Willem de Ridder. We were putting together a little, avant-gardish, one-shot sex magazine, with my diary excerpts and various photos. It was a labor of love, as we had no hopes of making much money from it, if any. We needed a typesetter, so we placed a help wanted ad in the local newspaper. Little did we know we'd hired an under-cover police woman, who cheerfully worked side by side with us for a month. To create something extra special for the climax, my friend, amputee centerfold, Long Jean Silver, came up from New York and we did a playful photo shoot, thoroughly enjoying each other's bodies, including her penetrating me with her sexy 16″ stump leg. I was delighted by our efforts. The moment our master-piece was completed, twenty-five state police (one-third of their entire department), along with our 'typesetter,' entered the house, guns drawn and pointed, wielding search and arrest warrants. Seems we had been under surveillance for a month, wire taps and all. We were charged with over a hundred felony counts combined: 'conspiracy to make and distribute obscene material,' 'sodomy,' and my personal favorite, 'conspiracy to commit sodomy.' In Rhode Island, sodomy is defined as 'an abominable, detestable act against nature,' which is apparently what some folks consider sex with amputees. My experience with Jean felt loving and liberating, and I assure you, nature was not offended at all.

We were thrown into freezing cold jail cells with no blankets or toothbrushes for forty-eight hours, treated like murderers by police officers and portrayed that way by the press. We gained comfort by planning a massive demonstration with hundreds of amputees and people in wheelchairs on the steps of the courthouse and by making up our own lyrics to famous protest songs like 'We Shall Overcum.'

Finally we were released on bail. Our friends in New York threw a benefit for us to raise funds to pay our lawyers, William Kunstler and Paul DeMaio. It was of course a sex party, held at Plato's Retreat (Manhattan's infamous sex club). The who's who of the sex world was there. Mickey even invited several vice offi-cers from the Rhode Island police department and they came (no pun intended) and even paid for their tickets. (A week later internal affairs held an investigation and some were suspended from their jobs!) Paul DeMaio, who was also a judge at the time, came, and almost got thrown off his bench after his photo appeared on the front page of the *Providence Journal* surrounded by a bevy of unauthorized women.

Eventually all our charges were dropped except for poor Mickey Leblovic's, who was found guilty of two counts of conspiracy to publish and distribute obscene material, and was sentenced to four years in prison (he served eighteen months). Now that's truly obscene! It was totally unjust. I was never able to recover my seized belongings – all my favorite sex toys, my bras and panties, the dog's leash, my toothbrush, a box of Tampax, my douche bag, or my personal nude snapshots of a lover who happened to be a New York City police officer. (He got in big trouble at his job. Oops.)

The arrest only fueled the flames of my desire to help make the world a more sexually mature and compassionate place. I continued to explore the vast frontiers of sexuality and to share and document my experiences and findings with explicit films, photography, writing and performance. However, being in jail did scare the shit out of me (although in actual fact, I got horribly constipated), so I took refuge in the art world where surprisingly I was made to feel quite welcome and found that I could be more myself and have a more eclectic aesthetic. There was much more creative freedom, less censorship, and more legal protection. For example, in various prestigious art theaters, I did a performance art piece where I inserted a speculum and invited the audience members to line up and each individually have a look at my cervix with the aid of a flashlight. Then I followed it up with a beautiful 'sacred sex magic, masturbation ritual.' If I had done the same thing at 42nd Street's Show World Center, not only would the audience not have liked or appreciated it, but I would have quickly been arrested, found guilty of breaking some silly law, and could possibly have gone to jail.

Of course artists do have their legal battles as well. There was never any problem anywhere in Europe, but in the US, every theater where I performed my controversial one-woman show *Annie Sprinkle, Post-Porn Modernist* had its lawyers standing by ready to bail me out of jail and fight the good fight. Although I came close many times, I was never arrested. Guess I had 'socially redeeming value' on my side. My name did get dragged through the mud on the US senate floor, by that adorable Senator Jesse Helms, in the debate over government funding for the arts. (All of the theaters where I had performed received some of the government's measly stipends.) For me, dealing with censorship and anti-sex laws is a way of life, something I deal with on a daily basis. I, and my peers, have experienced enormous amounts of harassment and abuse from bigoted, ignorant, sex-phobic people with their archaic, classist, misogynist laws.

There is a bright side. At a Chicago conference on Censorship in the Arts I fell madly in love with one of the lawyers who fought, and won, the 'NEA 4 case' against the National Endowment for the Arts. She was absolutely brilliant, charismatic, charming, and had a passion for women and their rights. We were lovers for almost a year.

Thus began my uncontrollable romantic obsession and intense sexual fetish for female lawyers. I absolutely melt next to someone wearing a grey pin-striped suit, with big hard law books, carrying a soft leather case overflowing with important briefs. I adore a lover who speaks Latin, can litigate, draft petitions, has the power to sue, and get someone out of a death sentence. Give me a stuffy, conservative office to make love in after hours. Give me a person who works out on the stairmaster of their mind, deconstructing and reconstructing contracts. Give me a lawyer whose job creates lots of stress and tension which I can lovingly and passionately relieve. Give me love letters on legal pads. Give me lesbian lawyer love.

I do hope that all my future brushes with the law, of which there will no doubt be many more, are primarily of a romantic, sensual nature. Lawyers do make the best motions.

Dear Friends and Lovers at 848

One of my favorite performance artists, Keith Hennessy, asked me to write something for a book he was editing with Rachel Kaplan, *More Out Than In: Notes on Sex, Art and Community*. For several years he and some friends had run a performance space (called '848' after its San Francisco address) where artists were free to explore the subject of sexuality if it came up in their work. Needless to say, the subject did come up, a lot, and it often created controversy. Keith hoped his book could address the controversies.

I wrote this shortly after I moved out of New York City, where I had lived and worked for twenty-three years. I moved to the country, gave myself a sabbatical, and the freedom to take a critical look at the things I had done. I needed to express what I was uncovering. After this personal process, my work/life became more well balanced, mature and integrated, albeit just a little less upbeat.

Dear Friends and Lovers at 848,

You surely must know that you folks at 848 are at the vanguard of the sexual evolution of this planet – the tip of the arrow. (I've traveled the world in search of the greatest sex experts, so I know.) Your combined experience, creativity and compassion is having a wide reaching and profound effect. I have learned a lot, been inspired, and grown through your community.

I have noticed that there is a lot of blind faith, even fanaticism, among sex radicals in the belief that all consensual sex is a totally positive thing (I was once one myself). Until recently, it seemed important to be wholeheartedly 'sex positive,' to defend, and encourage all promiscuity, all kinks and fetishes, all getting paid for sex, all group sex, etc. There were so many forces against our sexual choices. But my sense is that now lots of those battles have been won. We've reached a critical mass, and as Betty Dodson said recently, 'We've changed the world.' Perhaps there's no need to keep fighting for or defending something that we largely have and know to be true. This *modus operandi* has become obsolete.

For the past six months I have had the great luxury of taking some time to look back, to reflect, analyze and critique my personal sexual journey. Yes, I had a lot of fun, gave and received a lot of pleasure, and had a lot of great orgasms, but I have also come to see that I was sometimes quite naïve, very immature, and in denial about a lot of things. I'm realizing that some of the porn, prostitution, S/M and group sex I had 'in the name of love and sex positivism' wasn't necessarily all 'healing and enlightening,' but, on occasion, abusive to myself and others, and often perpetuating a totally dysfunctional, destructive, patriarchal model of sexuality. I now realize that I was often motivated more by a low self-image, the need for money, a desire for power, fear of intimacy, the need for attention, an addiction to intensity, etc. than I was aware of, or cared to admit.

As I begin to speak out about these realizations to my friends and colleagues, I am often met with resistance. Much of the beauty and uniqueness of the 848 community is that you are open to honest criticism, as shown by this publication. It is so precious to have a place to speak out about, and perform about, our 'mistakes,' doubts, hurts, angers, fears, bullshit and dislikes, and to feel free to be critical about all the stuff we've been so busy defending. How precious to have a place which is so sex positive that we can be 'negative.' Please continue to maintain a good balance.

With great respect and gratitude,

Annie Sprinkle

You've Come a Long Way Baby: Twelve Steps to Cure Sex Worker Burnout

Whether you are a prostitute, a stripper, a porn star or a sex workshop leader, a sex educator, artist or theater person dealing with issues of sexuality, you can experience what I call Sex Worker Burnout (SWBO). Society in general is not supportive of the above trades/careers/people. There is enormous judgement, deeply ingrained prejudices that we all have because we are raised with sex-negative messages. (Just as we are raised to be racist, homophobic, classist, etc.)

I've known hundreds of people in the sexuality field and I've never known one to be immune from bouts of SWBO. The symptoms vary: depression, problems in relationships, feeling like people want to drain your energy, low self-esteem, frustration, a feeling of being stuck, being overly emotional, hopelessness, self-destructive behavior, and more. It can last anywhere from one day to years. So I created this twelve-step program for myself and others to follow when needed.

Step 1: Admit you're burned out. This sounds easy, but it's actually the hardest step. Our egos, as well as our incomes, are invested in feeling good about our work. It's not easy to admit that you are a mess. Try to see it as an opportunity to grow.

Step 2: Take plenty of breaks and vacations from your work and spend some time in nature. Get some sun, fresh air, and smell the flowers. Boat rides are the best.

Step 3: Spend some time alone, do something relaxing or meditative. A long walk, and a candle-lit herbal bath can do wonders.

Step 4: Get in touch with your deep feelings. Learn to express them. Repressed emotions can create burnout.

Step 5: Get some therapy with a non-judgemental, professional therapist. It really does help to put things into perspective.

Step 6: Get together a support group of other sex workers with whom you can have sympathetic, honest communication. The best cure of all is to share your feelings with people who've had similar experiences.

Step 7: Take good care of your body. Eat well, exercise, get body work.

Step 8: Get your mind off work. Take a class, go to a funny movie. Hang out with children or old people.

Step 9: If at all possible, don't have sex for a while. Keep your clothes on for a change. I never thought I'd say this, but it really can help to recharge your battery.

Step 10: Be willing to make less money. Clean out your little black book. Learn to say NO!

Step 11: Learn other skills that can create alternative sources of income, so that when you need a break from sex work you'll have one. Periodically upgrade and expand your business(es).

Step 12: If your sex work burnout is chronic, get the hell out of the business, maybe it's time for a change. Sometimes getting out of the biz is really hard, but if there's a will there's a way.

Commentary: *A Labor of Love*

Annie Sprinkle is the modern-day love child of Jean Genet and Marcel Duchamp.

(*American Theater Magazine*, March 1999)

Fascination with the obscene body and its socially transgressive powers has haunted theatrical representation and social proxemics throughout Western history. Anxieties about performance invariably revolve around the tenuous boundaries between the sacred and the profane, actor and prostitute, tragedy and comedy. But if, as Aristotle argued, the purpose of theater as a civic activity was to arouse pity and terror through the public witnessing of a great man's fall, or his grotesque excesses, then, surely, in a highly ritualized patriarchal society in which only men performed at festivals, *pornographos* – the writing of or about prostitutes and their patrons – must have been a means of generating another kind of social discourse, one in which female presence and sexuality was no longer metonymic and in which knowledge about female eroticism was imitated and enacted by women, and passed down from one generation to another as an art form. In many ways, the tradition of female sexual initiation is the 'post' that Annie's post-porn modernism is reaching back for. As she delightedly acknowledged in a recent conversation with Linda Montano and Barbara Carrellas:

> my 'fans' are twenty-year-old female students getting degrees in Performance Studies, not men in trench coats ... There is performance art and there's the history of performance art, and the sexual knowledge that these twenty-year-olds have is far beyond what we ever had. They're going to be far better lovers than we ever were.[1]

Annie is dead serious when she claims that without prostitution, society would not function as well as it does. She should know. In a recollection of her early brushes with the law, Sprinkle playfully reveals herself as the proverbial crack in the signifying system of puritan capitalism. As Jean Genet suggested over forty years ago in his play *The Balcony*, the law is sustained – and indeed justified – by the image of the criminal. The performance of prohibited desire is endlessly preserved in prohibition. Like Sprinkle, who passionately understands the politics of labor behind the erotics of fantasy, Genet's peep-hole drama explores the slippery dialectics of illusion and reality, power and submission. In one of many insulated chambers within Madame Irma's House of Illusions, a mock judge derives sexual and existential gratification from the phony confession of a hired female thief. Other functionaries in disguise also perform their chosen roles so credibly that they eventually replace the nomenclature outside the Bordello's walls. Social identity is shown by Genet to be nothing more than a labor of disguise carefully constructed, the tender heart of mimesis. Madame Irma formally closes Genet's ritual drama with a direct address to the audience. As the actress flips the auditorium lights on, she wryly concludes, 'You must now go home, where everything – you can be quite sure – will be falser than here . . .,'[2] reconfirming that all of our identities are created by an outside source and shattering our final illusion: that what we were watching was only a play.

By breaking down the boundaries between performer and spectator, and blurring distinctions between art and life, Genet boldly fulfilled part of what performance art would make possible three decades later: the unmediated performance of the obscene and criminalized body, the urgent retributive forces of gender, race and sexuality speaking back to the status quo. In this venue, 'the voyeuristic narrative of traditional live theater is [completely] deconstructed, leaving the audience exposed to the fearful proximity of the performer and the . . . consequences of [its] own desires.'[3] Annie Sprinkle's self-consciously prostituted body further radicalizes her position on stage. As Bell puts it:

Prostitutes are 'spectacles' in patriarchal discourse and much of feminist discourse; their performance moves toward deconstructing female sexual spectacle. From their position as the carnival other in the dominant representation of the female body, from their position as a pornographic body, prostitute performance artists displace, transcode, and overwrite this representation. The effect of bringing the pornographic genre into art space is a displacement of both pornography and art through their intertext.[4]

As Linda Williams points out, the rhetoric of prohibition serves only to make the slippage between 'ob/scene' performance and 'on/scene' performativity more fluid. Williams invokes the exhibitionistic manner with which senator Jessie Helms responded to Robert Mapplethorpe's NEA-funded photographs, in 1989, on the senate floor. Waving copies of the photographs before his colleagues, he exclaimed:

> Look at the pictures! Look at the pictures! Don't believe the *Washington Post*! Don't believe *The New York Times*! ... I'm going to ask that all the pages, all the ladies, and maybe all the staff leave the Chamber so that senators can see exactly what they're voting on.[5]

Helmes' call for the male elite to remain in the senate chamber to 'look' at Mapplethorpe's images amplifies the tradition of an exclusively male privilege of and structure for secretly viewing the explicit or criminalized body. It is a well-documented fact that pornography as a separate category did not exist until the ninetenth century, when lawmakers throughout Europe ostensibly sought to protect a predominantly white, middle-class female population from sexually explicit material and – by extension – knowledge of their own sexuality. Annie's essays are cultural documents that chronicle the possibility of a kinship system of sexual knowledge through a female line.

Notes

1. Annie Sprinkle, interview with the author, Poughkeepsie, New York, April 2000.
2. Jean Genet, *The Balcony*, in *The Harcourt Brace Anthology of Drama*, ed. W.B Worthen (Orlando: Harcourt, 1996), p. 514.
3. Shannon Bell, *Reading, Writing and Rewriting the Prostitute Body* (Bloomington and Indianapolis: Indiana University Press, 1994), p. 139.
4. *Ibid.*, p. 14.
5. Linda Williams, *Hard Core: Power, Pleasure, and the 'Frenzy of the Visible'* (Berkeley: University of California Press, 1999), p. 285.

Part III

Interviews: A Movable Feast

Annie Sprinkle and Veronica Vera are The High-Heeled School of Journalism. Photo: © J.-M. Guyuax.

Annie's Breakfast with Veronica Vera: The Art of Sex Work

Veronica Vera and I have been best friends for many years. We have worked on hundreds of projects together. Presently she is Dean of her own unique creation, Miss Vera's Finishing School for Boys Who Want to Be Girls and the author of a book by the same name (www.missvera.com). We had our breakfast in cyberspace.

VV: Good morning, my darling. I'm just waking up and having my morning coffee. My favorite ritual of the day. What a treat to be sharing it with you.

A: My pleasure. Let's see. What year did we meet?

VV: We met in 1980, which means that this year marks the twentieth anniversary of our friendship. In the beginning, there was R. Mutt Press, that group of artists, writers and provocateurs that included Spider Webb, Charles Gatewood, Marco Vassi, V.K. McCarty, Michael Perkins, all of whom called Woodstock, NY, a sort of second home. I was a newly liberated Catholic girl. My mother had just died the year before. It was an experience that changed my life and put me in touch with my own mortality. I had decided to leave my straight business-world job, where I had accumulated a small nest-egg, and pursue my dreams to be a writer. You had just come back from Italy and two years under the influence of the great artist Willem de Ridder, who, of course, you were fucking too. Fucking seemed always to be part of the process of communication. I had gone to Marco, the great writer and self-described 'avatar of Eros,' to learn more about S/M, a discipline that was a natural complement to my early religious indoctrination. You were fucking Charles, modeling for him and getting photography lessons, to boot. We were all in Charles's comfy living room with the wood-burning stove. You said you had something to show us and the next thing I knew we were being showered, so to speak, with brilliantly colored European sex magazines. Many were much more expensively produced than American mags, people in rubber with enema tubes (all very neat and pristine), some interesting farm animals. You were so enthusiastic. I was very impressed and remember thinking, 'This is a very dedicated pornographer.' I guess you responded to my enthusiasm, because we hit it off immediately.

In the beginning, I still had an income and I did not have to work too hard. I wrote for magazines like *Penthouse Variations*, *Adam*, I was a member of *Stag*'s Pussy Posse, but quit because the slant was too low-brow. I always liked to class things up. And I know that you liked that about me. You were hitting the bumpy burlesque trail, capitalizing on your movie fame and introducing 'Strip Speak' where you would actually communicate with the audience, rather than simply take off your clothes. I accompanied you a few times. There was a safety for me in that. I could jump up on stage with you or jump into the Polaroid photos you took with your fans, slip out of my conservative skirt and sweater set and get nearly naked without committing to actually being a porn star. There was still a lot of Catholic girl in me. We were both into audience participation. It was fun getting horny guys, who might normally just sit quietly in their seats playing with themselves, to jump up on stage, take off their shirts and play with us.

In 1988 we would do a very similar performance at the Kitchen in *Carnival of Sleaze*, only this time we played to a mixed-gender audience, and got great reviews in an officially sanctioned 'art space.' Except for the curator's choice of the title, this seemed to be much more up our alley.

A: What were some of the things we did together? We made a feature film with Gerard Damiano at my apartment, called *Consenting Adults*, which was perhaps the first 'gonzo' sex film, in which everyone got to do what they wanted to in their sex scene.

VV: I had dubbed your apartment 'The Sprinkle Salon' after one 'event.' What a magical place it was. One day when I was about to leave, you invited me to stay for tea. You had invited Gerry Damiano, to discuss an idea you had to make an X-rated movie in which everyone would play themselves. That spot of tea was like the potion that led Alice to Wonderland, for I was soon starring opposite you in my first X-rated movie. I wasn't supposed to perform sex in the film, I would just be an interviewer and when the spirit moved me, I would flash my newly pierced nipple. That changed the day you called me into the sex scene with you and Michael Cycle. It was Michael's first time on camera and he was intimidated. You thought fast and invited me to join you, thinking that with two women on his hands he wouldn't have time to worry about his erection and would rise to the occasion. It worked like a charm. Afterward, I looked at my reflection in your bathroom mirror: well, I thought, I had sex on camera and was not struck by lightning. I felt so free and more committed to the film and my career than ever. I use that experience in my performance piece, *Bare Witness*. The last line of the scene illustrates the conflict in my mind as I went down on you and Michael Cycle entered me from behind: 'Don't let mommy see me, don't let daddy see me, don't let God see me ... Let the whole world see me, I'm a fucking movie star!' It was a real turning point in my life. In 1998 at the First World Pornography Conference that we both attended, I made the statement that I thanked God I took that step.

You know, Annie, what you did for me, sort of holding my hand through that process, helping me to confront my fear and desire is what I do now with my students. Many of them have never seen themselves totally transformed into females until they look in the mirror at the Academy. I pray that in each case, it is as liberating as it was for me.

A: We hostessed many events at the Sprinkle Salon: an evening with Fakir Musafar (the father of the Modern Primitive culture), an evening with Kutira (Oceanic Tantra teacher), Ecstasy Breathing with Jwala. We co-directed *Rites of Passion*, a couples-oriented erotic video produced by Candida Royalle. Did many Sluts and Goddesses workshops together.

VV: 'Events!' The word still gets me excited and always will.

A: Remember when phone sex hit? We made a million of those one-minute phone recordings for *Partner Magazine*? Some of those were definitely conceptual art!

VV: That was the best gig of all time. $50 a minute. We ad-libbed the entire script. The last 20 seconds was lots of heavy breathing followed by a big 'O.'

We made our magazines, like *Annie Sprinkle's ABCs of Sexual Lust and Deviation*, we printed newsletters ... In 1986, we began working together as a photojournalist team. *Penthouse* was our main client. You and I were on our way to an assignment in

Philadelphia, Jennifer Blowdryer, who would later create a performance series called *Smut Fest*, was along as your photo assistant. We decided we needed a name for our collaboration and came up with 'The School of High-Heel Journalism.' We not only documented the stories, we very much were the stories. In Los Angeles where we covered the adult film awards we dressed in crinolines and wore sexy T-shirts on which you had printed 'Retired Porn Star.' We were definite photo ops. I wanted to go to Brussels to cover the Second World Whores' Congress and convinced Jack Heidenry at *Penthouse Forum* to send us. We were the only journalists to also be delegates. Can you believe that prostitution is still against the law?

When I decided to testify in Washington for freedom of expression in 1984, in what would later become part of the Meese Report, you volunteered to document the event with your camera. You didn't want to testify you said, because you didn't want to speak in front of all those people. You, who would later be famous for your 'Public Cervix Announcement.' 'Document everything' became our motto. Documentation meant we could make our own interpretations. It also felt like we had control, even if we didn't. There was freedom in that structure.

A: Willem de Ridder affectionately called us 'artholes,' and gave us enormous support and encouragement. What were those gifts that he gave us that were so key to our careers and who we are today?

VV: There are few people as generous as Willem de Ridder. Willem told us to think of everything we did as art. But not the stodgy museum or academic kind of art, art that was alive, art that exuded body fluids, art that was fun. Willem made himself totally accessible to us. He was never too tired to help with a project. *Love '83*, the magazine that we made with him in that year, is still my very favorite. When I was struggling over a piece about my earliest memories of masturbation and sexual guilt for that magazine, I feared that my struggle meant I wasn't ready to write about it or it really should not be written. Willem advised, 'When you are sweating, when the pen is shaking in your hand, these are the pieces that are really worth writing.' That piece has had a long and varied life span. He was the inspiration and the narrator behind The Sprinkle/Vera Salon, our short-lived venture into public-access TV. He was also very respected in Holland and invited us to participate as visiting artists in the Holland Festival and all the while, Willem stayed hot and horny. I think we both met Willem at the perfect time to hear his message. Later that message would be reinforced by Linda Montano. I will be forever grateful to Willem for setting me on the right path as an artist.

A: What makes our sex work more like artwork than other sex workers make? What makes our artwork more like sex work than other artists make?

VV: We are artists and sex is our medium.

A: What do you think made us unique in the world of sex work? In the world of art?

VV: We have each other, and our idealism.

A: Do you think we actually made an impact on the world? What world/s?

VV: The world has responded to us, sometimes with approval, sometimes with disapproval. I think the great challenge is something you attributed to something Carolee Schneeman told you, that we need to 'guard our meanings.' The world is always ready to make its own interpretations and simplifications, we need to stay vigilant that what we mean is clear, especially to ourselves. I see that with my academy project. It is not just about a man in a dress, it is about personal liberation and empowerment. It is about assimilating a consciousness. It is about changing the world.

A: Do you think we hid behind the art label? Why did we want to be seen as something besides the usual sex workers? Why didn't we do our porn and sex work the mainstream commercial way?

VV: The art label is like the emperor's new clothes, not much room to hide. We go beyond sex work because our intention is to go beyond an individual encounter, we want to turn on the world. We don't mind being publicity hounds.

We didn't do our porn and sex work in the mainstream commercial way because a) it was too often limited by the greedy sophomoric attitudes of the men in charge; b) we didn't need the money that bad; c) we had each other – and we found others with whom to collaborate. Collaboration is so important.

The women of Club 90, with whom we performed *Deep Inside Porn Stars* at the Franklin Furnace and with whom we have had an ongoing porn-star support group these past fifteen years, have been especially important.

A: Yes, Club 90 was majorly empowering for us.

When we were in the porn mainstream, subversively making our porn into art, do you think the 'porn fans' liked our unusual take, didn't notice it, or just put up with it because they liked my tits and your ass?

VV: They loved our enthusiasm above all, but the tits and ass sure got their attention.

A: When I'm a visiting artist lecturing on college campuses, I inevitably get asked the question, 'When you were working in porn and prostitution, weren't you just contributing to the patriarchy? Young women are commodities for men's pleasure, and you helped perpetuate bad, misogynist habits.' What do we say to that?

VV: 'Eat me!' Whoops, I guess I'm getting hungry. What I have learned is to forget about the woman I am 'supposed' to be and be the woman I am ... now, shall it be Shredded Wheat or a doughy, warm, sensuous bagel?

Lunch at the Art/Life Institute: A Conversation with Linda M. Montano, Barbara Carrellas, and Gabrielle Cody

It was a lovely spring day. Linda Montano made a delicious potato soup and Indian spiced tea. We brought chocolate chip cookies and apple pie with whipped cream. After we got all our personal news and gossip out of our systems, Linda led us in a relaxing meditation. Then we put on the tape recorder to chat about our many years of collaboration.

GABRIELLE CODY: Annie, how long have you and Linda known each other?

ANNIE SPRINKLE: Well, I met Linda when she was in her yellow year. That's how I count. How many years is that? Red, Orange, Yellow, 85, 86 . . . 87. That's fourteen amazing years, plus maybe about a hundred past lifetimes.

BARBARA CARRELLAS: Annie and I met at the New York Healing Circle in 1988.

AS: I met Barbara a year after I met Linda. Barbara and I were lovers for about three days. She showed me where my G-spot was.

BC: When did you do Summer Saint Camp with Linda?

LINDA MONTANO: That was the summer of 87 wasn't it? In 1984, on December 8th, I began a performance titled, *14 Years of Living Art*, based on the Chakras or Hindu energy centers inside the body. Having studied meditation with my guru, Shri Brahmananda Saraswati, founder of Ananda Ashram, Monroe, NY, I always found his teachings on the Chakras very exciting and I wanted to experience each energy center intensely, so I concentrated on one each year wearing the color associated with the Chakra and performing private disciplines which focused my attention on the Chakras' qualities. Two aspects of the experience

Linda Montano, Barbara Carrellas and Annie Sprinkle at the Art/Life Institute, Kingston, New York. Photo: © Gabrielle Cody.

were public: my seven-year, monthly visits to the New Museum, where I did one-to-one Art/Life counseling with visitors who came to my window installation, and the two-week Summer Saint Camp that I conducted for seven years at the Art/Life Institute, Kingston, NY. Luckily Annie and Veronica Vera saw my ad for Summer Saint Camp in Franklin Furnace's bathroom and came to the Art/Life Institute, and we had an incredible, intense meeting of minds, hearts, and bodies and intentions and friendship. For each of the seven days, we explored one of the Chakras; it was friends being together, that's what the Summer Saint Camp was about. And it began a love that has grown, and I consider Annie beyond the beyond. There are no words for our friendship.

AS: I first learned about Linda Montano in my History of Performance Art class (with Cathy O'Dell at the School of Visual Arts) and was totally turned on. I did my term paper on 'Sex in Performance Art,' and I included Linda because I thought that her work was incredibly erotic, in a subtle way. During that first fertile week, the seeds were planted for what was to become my first one-woman show, *Post-Porn Modernist*. Linda baptized me an artist. And I fell madly in love with her. After my parents, Linda has been my biggest influence, and my greatest inspiration. She's absolutely hands down my favorite artist. Whenever I see something she's done or written or performs I'm just touched beyond words to the depth of my soul, in every pore.

LM: Well, on that theme of collaboration, it feels like there is a Siameseness with us and Barbara and all of us. We extend each other. Annie permissioned me to go into areas that were locked and forbidden and tabooed. And the encouragement to sacralize the first and second Chakras with her, with her blessing, basically changed my work considerably and my direction. So it's really a sisterhood that was born. And Annie's gift is collaboration and being a community maker and a taboo breaker, and it has changed my life. I can't take seven steps without seeing the influence of her work. One of the most outlandish, the most wild, groundbreaking things we did together, the three of us, Annie, Barbara and I, is that we stormed Texas with the unspeakable, with material that's absolutely sacred but dangerous.

BC: Was it performance art or was it just a group live sex show?

AS: That was the MetamorphoSex project.

LM: I feel every woman on the planet would benefit from the kinds of places that Annie and Barbara are able to take them, and it's about not just performance, it's about ritual and it's about initiation, which are central to our growth and to our passage to the next step of maturity. And until our bodies and our costumes and needs are ritualized and initiated by wise women, there is going to be a lot of misdiagnosed, and misapplied performance.

AS: Do you remember when we went to the Hell Fire Club [an S/M club]? What did we do there? Somebody wrestled but I can't remember, was it you and me, or Susun Weed and Barbara?

BC: I remember liquid Crisco oil.

LM: Remember the human pony?

AS: I delighted in taking my guru, my mother superior, Linda, an ex-nun, to places she wouldn't normally go. I took her to a friend of mine's whorehouse, and on a tour of 42nd Street peep shows and porn palaces. I took you to Plato's Retreat, a huge swing club . . .

LM: That was my favorite. And then you took me to the lap dance place. And I was very like: 'Annie what should I do now? Should I sit? Should I stand up now?' One of the things I'll never never never forget – I think it was Plato's Retreat – it was walking in and having a waft of red energy, but it had no thorns in it, everyone was there consenting to be there. Everyone was there for the same purpose. It was so hot and so heavy.

AS: Just as I took Linda into the underworlds of the first and second Chakra, she gave me permission to go into the heart Chakra, and my more spiritual, priestess personas, and to bring those into my work/life. Which is what I think took me out of commercial sex work, into a much broader world. I went from a one-Chakra world to a seven-Chakra world. That was tremendously liberating for me and deeply satisfying. She took me to a Zen Buddhist monastery, to the university she was teaching at, and to the Ananda Ashram. We spent about nine New Year's Eves at Ananda. We did a ritual every New Year's Eve, sometimes with vibrators and sometimes without. She's been my guide into all kinds of important life stuff. Now she's guiding me into the worlds of menopause, financial frugality and death.

LM: And we can't forget the years you would invite not only me, but four hundred thousand, million, trillion of the most unusual, wonderful, free beings in the world, who came through your doors in New York City. It was extraordinary. It was two rooms and a bathroom and a small kitchen that became the richest, most creative rooms in the world. They were temples, they were studios, they were photo studios, they were performance studios, they were the center of your writings, of your photography, of your love, of your people, and a permission to celebrate life. One of Annie's incredible talents is organization. And an ability to transform spaces through four ounces of effort, but tremendous energy. One of Annie's teachings is 'magnificence of heart,' compassion.

BC: Your apartment would be littered with newsletter makings. And then you'd go, 'Oh sorry I forgot to mention I have a photo session this afternoon.' Suddenly, the bed would come apart, pieces of plywood were going down the hall. So inherently theatrical! And there always seemed to be enough stage-hands. Then, the more people arrived, you realized Annie's attention did not become diluted, but rather the whole experience was enhanced. And even if you didn't particularly like someone ... you'd realize they had something to offer you ... You never left without learning something, or having a creative idea.

AS: Well ... Linda of course introduced me to the idea that life could be art, and life could be performance, and I think that was important key information for me.

BC: Linda, let's face it, you're one of the wackiest artists who has ever lived. And wacky means anything can be art. You gave us permission to be artists. Annie, I've never seen you cry as hard, laugh as hard, feel as cosmically light or physically dense as I have when you are in Linda's presence. And I've seen you absolutely tear your guts out working with her, and float working with her. It's such a big experience for you, that it seems to take in all of your being.

AS: Yes. She spins all of my Chakras.

LM: Transgressive people doing transgressive work. I don't know if I could come under that category, but I know Annie and Barbara do. And it's a ministry, it's a sacred calling. And in India they would be honored as those saints that touch the Tantric world of opposites, where there is no good or bad, there is just the calling. And it's been at a price, a very, very high price. And we all go back to our blood families, and we pull out those personas that we have to pull out to be around those people, and then we integrate them back in and go back out and do the calling or the ministry.

AS: I think that our work together has not been focused on career or money or whatever. It's really been using sexuality as a theme to help us all grow and learn. In the workshops and performances we facilitated together for ten years we saw some incredible magic, beauty, truth, acceptance, transformations . . . so rich. . .

BC: I think because the trust between us is very strong.

AS: Barbara, let's talk about your background.

BC: I went into theater when I was fourteen. Because it was erotic, it was powerful, it changed the way people felt and acted. I was always drawn to doing plays with sex in them. Tennessee Williams was my absolute favorite because of all of that smoldering heat. I was trained at Trinity Square Rep Company before there was a conservatory, when you just went and soaked it up. Fast-forward in time. I had a business where I was general managing Broadway shows. At first we were doing a lot of 'high art' in commercial theater. We premiered Wendy Wasserstein's *Uncommon Women*, *Cloud Nine* and *A Coupla White Chicks* and the Broadway musical *Nine*. As the 1980s went on and the big British invasion created mega-musicals, the objective was to dazzle not to move people. And by 1988, I had come to the end of a chapter when I was the executive producer of Colleen Duhurst and Jason Robards in *Ah Wilderness*, and *Long Day's Journey*.

1988 was a pretty dark autumn. AIDS took many of my theater friends. I had been working with Louise Hay's philosophies for some years and I found this group based on her work. Bing bang boom, I'm at the New York Healing Circle and this wonderful, childlike spirit with red hair and something fluffy and polka-dotted caught my attention: 'Annie Sprinkle!' I knew her because I was a porn fan. We got to know each other better at Joseph Kramer's Tantric Group Rebirthing ritual, where you breathe rhythmically for three hours straight, at the end of which you tense your whole body, and let go. The Big Draw orgasm was very, very hot.

Annie was doing her *Post-Porn Modernist* show at the Harmony

Burlesque. I went and I thought, 'That's it! That's what I want! That's what I haven't seen in so long, that's what I'm looking for, that's what we should be doing.' Everything changed. January of 1990, the show was being presented at The Kitchen. I went as often as I could to help. For instance, Annie's altar wasn't rolling on stage properly. So I invited the owner of one of the huge Broadway scene shops to come see this wonderful show. The next day he delivered free casters that made the altar work. I would watch the audience. Literally guys with AIDS would walk in leaning on people, and leave under their own steam.

I left my general management firm, and set up shop with another woman [Denise Cooper], and in 1991 we produced *Post-Porn Modernist* in a New York run commercially. We started managing a handful of performance artists. It was clear that artists like Annie couldn't expect any funding from the government without hideous strings attached. It became my intention to help Annie and artists like her: Lipsynkca, Miss Coco, Shelly Mars, Penny Arcade. I learned how to help artists become commercial successes, if they were ready for it.

I couldn't believe the effect *Post-Porn Modernist* had. Annie was getting offers for a lot of gigs. She was trying to do it all herself and needed help. For me, it was really important that *Post-Porn Modernist* really look right. So that when she was showing her cervix or peeing or masturbating, which are scary things that can look very dirty, it all looked theatrically professional.

AS: Barbara negotiated excellent contracts for me ... She was great at getting really good money. She brought me up to a professional level.

BC: Annie brought me here to Linda. I was terrified to ask Linda if I could come to Summer Saint Camp, because I was not an artist, I was just a manager. Annie got me my artist back. She helped me get my courage to ask Linda, who said 'yes.'

What was really rewarding was watching Annie make that transition into believing she could act, and becoming a heartfelt actress. There were points in *Post-Porn Modernist* when things were happening 100 per cent in the moment. And others that she never could have done six times a week if she hadn't learned to act.

AS: I didn't know what the fuck I was doing.

LM: I would like to ask a question. How do you feel, as artists, that we can affect or effect the need of young women to become initiated without guidance? And how do you feel that performance art ... how can we head our work in the direction of even a more cross-generational healing?

I'm thinking of those who are called to make gestures that are particular to their own genetic and/or personal evolution and of when they are taken out of context and imitated by another generation, without either the confines and/or the safety. Is there a way we can 'Take Back the Night' in terms of what we've put out? How can we keep it sacred for those who will be misled by not seeing it correctly?

BC: In other words, why did you lose your teaching job and tenure? Someone who didn't see *MetamorphoSex*, or maybe just heard about it, thinks we were doing something we weren't, and they are going to try doing the same thing, but they didn't have any idea what it really was about. And then it becomes a live sex show.

AS: We have to let them make their mistakes. I did a visiting artist presentation at NYU yesterday. This student comes up to me at the end and she says, 'Yesterday I did a dance piece to your video *Zen Pussy* and no one will speak to me any more.' She was devastated. I gave her my phone number immediately, and said, 'Call me, I'm here to support you.' I've made plenty of similar kinds of 'mistakes' in the past. We learn from them.

LM: That's absolutely true. But I think what I'm addressing here is that they're going into places that they may not be ready for, or for the responsibilities of having gone where they went. Or have the strength to take some of the censorship of where they've gone. Or have the maturity to ...

AS: But that happens in porn and prostitution all the time.

LM: OK. One thing is, I have some reluctance to go the San Francisco Art Institute this semester because of a particular incident that a professor had in his class that became a kind of talk-show controversy. I am really at a place in my post-menopausal stage of life – and it's either coming from proximity to blood family or a complete closing down of all permission slips, or a punishment of myself for not having any kids, and then overindulging them in strict morals – that I don't know what I would say if I went and did something at the Art Institute and saw some of those people. I don't know if I'd say 'Let's stop now.' Or 'Bravo.' Or 'God, you still have your job.' Or 'What is this all about.' Or 'Let's do it differently so we can initiate ourselves differently, so we don't have the consequences of censorship for having explored real time, real space, real bodies, real flesh and real issues.'

AS: You're talking about the '**** factor.' Gaby, that's a phrase we coined to describe something like Murphy's Law, but it's specifically people oriented. It's about when people throw a big wrench into the works.

We did a workshop and there was a woman named **** who seemed to have had a wonderful, positive time. Six months later, after talking with what must have been a very sex-negative therapist, she decided our work had not been a good thing for her, and she felt that she had gone too far. She sent a very accusatory letter to everyone who had been in the workshop. We had created such a safe space and gave the women plenty of choices. But the work could be challenging. So later this woman freaked out and felt she had been exploited and violated. I was devastated. So, we retired our wonderful project in which twenty-four women were transformed for ever for the better. To continue the project seemed too huge a responsibility and risky. And it had been the best thing we had ever done together.

LM: I'm also addressing a call to future permissions, for me and for all of us, that if we are true to the calling, then we're willing to take risks even when we're in the presence of our non-community. We have to be extremely strict with our futures and proceed according to the truth, and take the consequences of our choices. Every action produces a reaction. What can we live with? What can we risk?

BC: ****'s change of heart affected Annie deeply. I had taught so many sex workshops at that point I was used to the fact that there are a few people who want to be right and others who want to be happy.

LM: I think these **** factors are sacred clowns, and I guess I'm calling to myself for more courage. To not be frightened by the clown, the Giuliani clowns, the police clowns, the censorship clowns, the lawsuit clowns . . .

GC: The academic clowns.

LM: Yeah. I had a hard time. I'm trying not to whoop my muse into submission or silence. And yet, also evolve into the next step which may not look like what I've done before. I'm not sure if that's coming from damage control or evolution of vision, or pure cowardice. I think it's the computer. What has happened is that fathers and grandfathers are hanging out in places that their grandchildren and nieces and nephews are hanging out in in real time, real space, and real flesh, and real issues. And the incumbent shame of persona-change chat rooms, diversions into what they consider deep-down morally destructive to themselves and the culture, is then transposed. So I think people are working on Annie Sprinkle's level, but they're doing it at different times, different places, with different permissions. The ones who are doing it in real time, and obviously have been taught by her how to work that way, are up for a certain level of censorship.

AS: The fact that I could be invited to go to NYU as a visiting artist and show a bunch of porn, and get paid for it, blows my mind. I couldn't do that even five years ago. It would be too controversial. Now it seems there's far less controversy. When I came on stage at NYU, these twenty-year-old girls were applauding wildly. That is shocking, because I come from a place where it was old guys in raincoats applauding. My audience is now twenty-year-old girls! They may spend more time on their computer. But they're doing sex research. Maybe they won't be performance artists, or sex workers, but it will happen on Internet sites. It's going to take different forms.

I have a question. As we get more well known, how do we stay humble and modest, and not get self-absorbed and stuck in our own PR legend?

LM: Visit your mother more. Blood family is humbling.

BC: I seldom get fed up with people who are searching for something higher. Annie you're on a quest, on a mission. When you do something 'for yourself' it winds up helping two hundred people.

AS: Thank you from the bottom of my heart. Without Linda and Barbara, I would certainly not be in this Critical Performances book series. And Gaby, thanks for creating this opportunity. Perhaps we should each do a summation.

LM: I'm looking forward to more Art/Life adventures with this Catholic woman Barbara here, and this incredible soul sister Annie. We invite the readers to create, appropriate, beneficial, well-intentioned experiences in Art/Life that lead to higher consciousness.

BC: Annie keeps me dangerous. I hope she does the same for you.

GC: May I quote: 'You are dear, divine, and very very pure. Let no one, no thing, no ideal or idea obstruct you.'

AS: How do I lose twenty pounds of ugly fat? And can you pass the chocolate chip cookies please?

Dinner with Richard Schechner and Gabrielle Cody: She Wanted a Better Life

Richard Schechner talked to me about Annie as he prepared a delicious bouillabaisse on a warm summer evening in his New York City apartment.

GABRIELLE CODY: Let's start out with the very beginning of you and Annie. Going to the Triple Treat Theater with your class. Elie Fuchs quotes you as saying that what drew you to Annie at this event was the 'sophistication of her play with the audience.' And that what you were interested in was the exchange of gazes. What was it that was so exciting about that work?

RICHARD SCHECHNER: Well, this was a class called Liminoid Theater in New York. And the idea was to go to performances that were in one way or another not recognized, illicit, from the high-art point of view. Going to a wrestling match, some street stuff, and pornographic performance in Times Square. For the porn night, I divided the class into about four groups, each group picked a place they were going to go to.

I went to the Triple Treat Theater and Annie was doing Nurse Sprinkle, and I was expecting an ordinary porn show, whatever that might have meant to me, but I certainly wasn't expecting Annie's return gaze, self-consciousness or all of the things that I found there that were so extraordinary. I'll give you a couple of examples, because they were really funny. The audience was a down-and-out audience, this was the 2 am show, there were some people there, all men, and they were coming in 'out of the cold' in many different ways. There was one guy who was very overweight, I mean he could hardly get out of his chair, and at one point Annie says to him, 'I think you would like to fuck me,' and the guy says, 'Yeah, I really would.' And so she says, 'Why don't you come up here and give it a try?' So the guy kind of lumbers out of his chair, gets up on stage, and he didn't know what this meant exactly. She said, 'I can tell you're nervous, but Nurse Sprinkle has a solution, you don't have to use your thing, use my thing.' So she pulls out a water pistol and says, 'Why don't you make believe this is your cock and you can cum as far as this water pistol can shoot?' So she gets herself ready, and he squeezes it, and it just doesn't shoot. She says 'Oh, well this is a problem,' and from there she gets into Nurse Sprinkle mode, to help you with your problems. And she did several things like this, which nobody was laughing at except me and several of the students. The guys in there weren't particularly amused at being set up and sent up. In fact, this one guy didn't even know he was being set up.

She also did the business, 'I bet you want to look at me,' and they say 'yes,' and she subverts the gaze by giving them a magnifying glass. The whole idea of the pornographic gaze is anonymity, distance, to fulfill the fantasy. It's not medical, clinical, with the person you're looking at instructing you what to look at and what to see, and saying, 'Isn't that pretty, isn't that great.' Because it makes you have an identity and a relationship, when the whole point of that kind of pornography is that you're not having that kind of confrontation. So after the show was over, I was just blown away, by her presence and the fun of it. I said, 'I know you're not going to believe me, but I'm a professor at NYU, and these young people are my class,' and she's rolling her eyes, 'and I'm also a director at the Performing Garage and I'd like you to be in my play. I don't want your phone number, I don't want you to think I'm hassling you at all. Here's my card, here's my phone number, if you're interested you'll call me.' So she called and the rest is history. I think that's the first time she began to move into the art world in the formal sense.

GC: Alisa Solomon reviewed the *Prometheus Project*, and she, like other people, was confused by the connection you were drawing between the Io/Nurse Sprinkle figure and the issue of pornography, and Hiroshima and nuclear disaster. Now, what I had gleaned from what you were attempting to do is that you were talking about two kinds of impossibilities, two historical impossibilities. The impossibility of representing Hiroshima mimetically, the impossibility of representing the sexual female body in a way that isn't already over-determined. So you were talking about this merging of impossibilities. So you weren't really addressing

Annie Sprinkle in *The Prometheus Project*, directed by Richard Schechner, 1985, NYC. Photo: © Leslie Barany.

voyeurism. You were addressing what in a theatrical event could disrupt voyeurism, and would, should, deconstruct it.

RS: Right, exactly. It wasn't offering voyeurism. Again, I asked Annie to take further what she took still further when she did her famous Speculum show, the idea of going to the audience and asking them to look. You want to look? OK, then look! In the staging of the Annie section, it was Annie's show. There were four people, they were all dressed as men in raincoats, and they were parodying the voyeuristic audience, which I took right from Jill Dolan's 'desire in a trenchcoat.' They were a parody of that, but what I wanted to do was make the audience itself conscious of its seeing. And Annie would go to women as well as men, and what she was doing was deconstructing this whole idea of what it is you're seeing. With what eyes are you looking? And she sang a song that she had composed especially for the Garage show, 'I'll Fuck Anything That Moves,' and she had also given her slide show on the economics of pornography as she practiced it.

GC: On the one hand, Annie's never acknowledged herself as a victim of oppression, she's always taken this Benjaminian position as self-knowing commodity. Was she in the *Prometheus Project* to critique pornograpy? A lot of people felt the pornography was gratuitous.

RS: I think Annie was critiquing it profoundly. And part of Annie's critique is that she herself does not possess the pornographic body or attitude, in terms of whatever the mainstream is, she doesn't have that kind of body, she has a mind. And in a certain sense, her lack of the pornographic body, and her sense of humor, gives her a different niche. So to call her body the pornographic body is to misread what you're seeing. And how she plays with it. I never thought of her performance as pornographic. Annie was doing a take-off on it. That's why she was ready to step from porn to art. What was keeping her there was her salary, and her community. In other words, I think that where the anti-porn people misread is that they don't see that people are people. When I knew Annie and the group she was hanging out with, they were like circus performers, they formed a community, which didn't have respect from the regular acting community, and which focused in on themselves. Annie was, in a certain sense, a pioneer in gaining respect for some of those people.

GC: But what makes Annie's performances very powerful is the conjunction of the intimate and the social.

RS: Yes, her sense of irony is so highly developed that the body is explicit and obscene and ironic at the same time. I mean there she is, she's out there, you see her vagina, or whatever you want to look at, her breasts, and so on. So that in our culture, in the theater, that's explicitness. It's also obscene, because she's playing with the tropes of pornography which are about sexual arousal. But I don't think her shows are about arousal. They're about the deconstruction of arousal. The greatest one in that regard is where she's sucking all these dildos and cocks and playing the movie producer. She's upstage and at the foot of the stage are maybe forty dildos. Some of them very anatomically correct, and some of them not. And she says she's going to show you what it's like to make a porn movie. Over the tape she has some guy who is telling her what to do. And every once in a while, she interrupts the tape and explains what to do. It's both scary and hilarious at the same time. And totally unsexual, because the mechanics are shown in such an exaggerated way, and this guy is sweet-talking her, and at the same time gets angry at her, you know: 'You're getting paid here, what are you doing?' and it's totally anti-erotic. And at that point, what is explicit? Because all we're seeing is plastic, I mean she's fully dressed, and these things are plastic and very far away. But the speech is explicit, and also again it strips the fantasy. She also has a sense of history. If you try to think about what she is saying through the term 'Post-Porn Modernism,' she's attacking the idea of postmodernism even when accepting it. And she says that in that tradition she can show you pornography that's no longer pornography.

The so-called primitivism in twentieth-century art has been a long dialog of how to rationalize the erotic in art. And the pornographic may be one of the last elements of the erotic to resist rationalization. In other words, we know that the 'great artists' did erotic work. If they weren't so great they would call them pornographic paintings and drawings; in other words, the distinction between eroticism and pornography is very difficult to define. A lot of it is about marketing and context, a lot of it is about the thing itself. And constant mechanical reproduction is one mark of pornography, and many aspects of popular culture, so in that sense pornography is a part of popular culture. And is pretty well ingrained in it, in terms of video stores, and video distribution. It's also predominately a male preoccupation.

GC: Why do you think Annie Sprinkle is a figure worth studying?

RS: Two reasons. First she's representative. As anthropologists, sociologists, theorists, we have to be interested in what's representative. And then in and of herself she's a significant artist. Some artists are significant but they're not particularly representative. A whole bunch of popular culture is representative, but not particularly great art, but very worth studying. I think that her contribution as an artist is that she has expanded the boundaries of what can be talked about in terms of art. And she's been explicit about that. She's explicitly artful, let's put it that way. She doesn't need someone else to tell her that what she does is an art form. Which is what happens when you primitivize somebody. The poor native is making a mask and we think it's ritual, we put it on a wall and say it's great art. But they don't even have a word for it in their culture! But in Annie's case, one doesn't have to rationalize her, she rationalizes herself. And she's quite aware of what she's doing. And in that sense she puts herself squarely in the field of art. Art is an attention to structure, accomplished consciously, and it's also a comment on itself. In other words it's in dialog with other people trying to make those kind of structural and formal claims. That does not mean that art does not also have context and social meaning, etc. In so far as it enters into dialog with the rest of the world it deals with the political and social questions. Annie has always been interested in the formal questions, she's come at them from two points of view. From the point of view of the photographer – she's a very good photographer – and therefore of visual composition and irony. And from the point of view of the performer. Not the pornographer. I think she's only incidentally a pornographer. That happened to be the medium through which she performed for part of her life, but I can only assume that she didn't begin with the show I saw at Triple Treat Theater that night, that she'd been doing it for quite a number of years and therefore she had always had a reputation of being kind of edgy in that world. And had a conscious control over what she was doing. So pornography was her medium, but art was her true calling.

Annie's Dessert with Mae Tyme, an Anti-Porn Feminist

We are two women from different worlds with very different experiences. I have performed in, directed and produced pornography for twenty-five years. Mae Tyme has been anti-pornography for equally as long. We met at a lesbian video night several years ago. You might think that we'd be enemies, because we have such different viewpoints. Could we come together to record a conversation, share our ideas, and show that women of disparate backgrounds and beliefs can communicate and collaborate?

ANNIE: Don't you think it's so totally interesting to see people naked, or to watch them having sex?

MAE TYME: I used to play a game as a kid called Peeping Tom in my suburban neighborhood. I was forever peeking into people's windows. I hoped I would see somebody naked. I never did. It wasn't a sexual kind of thing, it was curiosity. All I saw was women cooking and doing dishes, and men watching TV or working in their garages.

A: I don't remember seeing any adults naked until I was seventeen, and saw my boyfriend. After that I was hooked. I wanted to see naked people all the time. I was instantly fascinated by genitalia. Here was an entire secret universe!

A year later I ended up in pornography and prostitution. I'm still busy looking at genitalia.

MT: I saw my grandmother naked quite a bit. It didn't involve sexual feelings. I loved watching her come out of the shower and put on her corset, and powder her face. It made me feel close and accepted. Later in college I always loved watching girls get dressed up for dates. I'm sure that some of that was sexual, but I didn't realize it at the time.

A: So, you are aware of people's basic desire to see other people naked. How did you get to be so anti-pornography?

MT: Seeing someone naked was always sort of serendipitous. It wasn't something I cultivated deliberately to get turned on, or to try to turn them on. It might have had a sexual result, but not a sexual purpose.

A: Hmmm, basically I don't see anything wrong with cultivating sexual excitement.

MT: I've been a lesbian since I was twenty-one. In my thirties, feminism came along. Then I moved into radical lesbianism. I have not related intimately with a male in I can't think of how many years. I have seen some males naked at nude beaches, and actually that has served to depowerize, demystify men. So when I feel oppressed by the patriarchy, I sometimes just conjure up some of the images I had of males on nude beaches and laugh.

A: Partly why I went into prostitution was that male genitalia was such a big mystery. Now I'm busy unraveling the female genitalia mystery.

MT: I remember a woman coming to a women's event and she showed slides of 'beaver.' It was hard for me to look at the photos. Even though I had been a lesbian for a long time and had been going down on them, and had been gone down on and saw them all the time. But looking at them in pictures was really icky to me.

A: Betty Dodson tells the story of being at a NOW conference about sexuality in the 1970s, where she did a slide show of vulvas. Half the women walked out.

MT: What feminists didn't take into account was that although most of us had done consciousness-raising and had intellectually looked at issues about sexuality and decided that we don't smell like tuna, and all this stuff, it was still hard to deal with the actual experience of touching our own vulvas, of looking at ourselves with speculums, and looking at pictures of 'down there.'

A: Don't you have any male friends?

MT: My consistent bonding and involvement with other women, especially lesbians, is so fulfilling, inspiring to me, that even if I felt OK about men, which I don't, I wouldn't have any time for them.

A: To me pornography is any photo, film or drawing that shows hardcore explicit sex. How exactly do you view pornography?

MT: As something that is overwhelmingly by, about and for men. It is a worldwide industry that generates gazillions of dollars every year from which women do not benefit.

A: In porn films female performers get paid a whole heck of a lot more than the male performers.

MT: I didn't know that. I've always viewed pornography as an aspect of oppression of women, not of our liberation. And I view the nuclear family pretty much that way too. So I've tried to develop a sexuality that isn't about men or what they want, but is entirely about women and how we relate to each other.

A: Would a typical sex magazine just totally turn you off?

MT: Yes. I am trying to learn what sex is about for a free and voluntarily participating woman. My view has been that all women that do pornography are either terribly misinformed, or they've been enslaved. You tell me that's not true at all. That being in porn can be liberating and profitable.

A: I agree that we all have a lot of programed ideas about what is sexy. There is plenty of room for porn to be more creative, experimental, feminist, and more erotic for women. But it's harder to create that than you might think. That's the challenge I love.

MT: If I were to make an erotic video it would probably be boring to someone else. I did have an experience of a lover of mine videotaping us making love, and then we watched it.

A: What. I'm shocked! YOU made porn?

MT: I didn't think of it as porn. It was deeply thrilling, because watching it made me remember the feelings and it was wonderful. If someone else watched it, they probably would be uninspired. We were lying down, holding each other, and moving together, with enormous sexual and love energy between us. There wasn't any sucking or licking, or fingers. There were no toes curling. Well, that's not true. My toes did curl. It certainly had nothing to do with costumes, lights, props, or plots.

A: Did you ever show it to anyone?

MT: No.

A: Oh come on, Mae. You could sell it! Think of the money you could make. The people you could inspire. You could pioneer a whole new genre.

MT: I talk about this only with other lesbians. It is very challenging for me to consider revealing this in a context where men have access to it, and where women might exploit it. It's giving personal information to the enemy.

A: If you were a communist, you probably wouldn't have a problem telling people you were a communist.

MT: Oh, but I would. You can be arrested, threatened, lose your job, things can happen to you if you say too much of your truth to the wrong people. As a radical lesbian I must exercise great caution not to compromise or endanger myself or my sisters. What lesbians do in bed is inflammatory. Lesbians have been assaulted and killed because of what we do sexually. I'm reading a book called *8 Bullets*, written by the survivor of a lesbian couple shot by a man on the Appalachian trail. One was killed. Men hate lesbians because we have sex and life without them.
    An aspect of porn that is so distressing is child slavery. Girl children – or women who are trying to look like girls – shaved, infantilized, tiny, etc. are used to entertain men who are basically getting off on trying to fuck little girls. Incest is the paradigm of patriarchy. The latest figure from the FBI, even, is that three out of four girls are sexually molested by the age of eighteen. How can we possibly discover our own sexuality when it has been conditioned into us since we are infants?

A: By learning more about sex. And by making our own porn. You realize that child pornography is the number one argument that is consistently used against all of us decent pornographers who are simply trying to make people feel good and turned on. There's maybe .01 per cent of porn made which involves children, and it is not readily available for sale. I challenge you to find any commercial child porn anywhere in the USA.

MT: Look at all the stuff on the Internet.

A: It doesn't exist.

MT: That's like saying the holocaust doesn't exist. They're busting men who are meeting kids on the Internet to try and have sex with them.

A: Yes, unfortunately that could be true. But the only nude picture of a twelve-year-old girl you can find on the American Internet was put there by the FBI to entrap pedophiles.

MT: I believe that child porn happens all the time. And your experience says it almost never happens!

A: It happens occasionally in some people's garages underground in a very illicit way, but not as a big commercial industry. This is the most difficult subject of all to talk about.

MT: In 1995, there was a big story when I was in Europe about two girls, ten and eleven years old, who had escaped from a porn ring. They'd been kidnapped. The porn ring was busted, and they discovered other girls who had been starved, beaten and enslaved.

A: That's horrible. But once I was making a little sex magazine with some friends, as a labor of love, not a big money-making thing. We unknowingly hired an undercover police woman to be our typesetter. The people whose house it was had two kids, who were not involved in any photographs. The parents made a living making magazines from pictures that people sent them. Twenty-five state police officers came into the house with guns drawn, arrested us and confiscated everything, from Tampax to the dog's leash. In the family photo album there was a photo of the two kids in the bathtub naked when they were three and five, the same photo every family has. The newspaper headline said 'INTERNATIONAL CHILD PORNOGRAPHY RING BUSTED.' The two kids were put in dreadful foster homes for several weeks, which really traumatized them. That's when I realized how much the press perverts the facts, and how sex-negative attitudes are used to hurt innocent people.

Every time I do a lecture at a college or a reading at a book store, with my good intentions, inevitably this scary topic about children being abused comes up.

MT: The same thing is used against lesbians. We are called child molesters. We point out over and over that most molestation of children and others is done by straight males.

A: I've been putting out sexually explicit images of myself for years. I know this sounds bizarre, but somehow it makes me feel safer.

MT: Being very out as a lesbian makes me feels safer. I think blatant is best.

A: Aren't you 'putting information into the hands of the enemy' by being an out lesbian?

MT: I'm out so that other dykes will recognize me. I don't do it to annoy men.

The truth is that you and I do view pornography very differently. You view it as an avenue to independence, joy, freedom, fun . . .

A: . . . education, harmony, a creative outlet, a safer world . . .

MT: I view it as reinforcing destructive sexual response patterns. If women get any joy and freedom from it, it's an accident.

A: I think you are a good teacher for me, because you have developed a type of sexuality that is more egalitarian, sensitive, subtle, less performative.

MT: You're a good teacher for me, because you are developing concepts of energy and teaching women about female ejaculation, about self-pleasuring, dispelling shame. But when it gets to be part of the porn industry, I absolutely view it as part and parcel of the patriarchy.

A: You cannot deny that there is an energetic/erotic/sexual/sensual/emotional exchange with virtually everything and everyone on a daily basis. People try to deny that, but denial only goes so far. It's a natural law of the universe and biologically programed. If a child sits on your lap and touches your hair it can feel very erotic. Some adults simply don't know how to handle the feelings.

Feminists say that rape is an act of violence, not an act of sex. I think it is also very violent sex.

MT: It doesn't have to do with sex. It is about power and dominance.

A: But it is still sexual.

MT: No. It's about fear and terror and coercion.

A: I agree. But it's also misdirected sexual energy.

MT: Let's go back to the kid who plays with the hair. The kid likes the feel of the hair. The adult likes having its hair touched. That is freedom and exploration. But if the adult makes that activity something else, like 'come up on daddy's lap, honey, touch daddy's hair, honey,' that is training the child to provide sexual pleasure for the adult. That is inappropriate and wrong.

A: So we need to train people how to be . . .

MT: . . . sexual in joy and freedom and love without imposing or coercing others and without using it for dominance.

A: I'm there with you. When I worked as a prostitute, I specialized in handicapped . . .

MT: . . . differently abled.

A: Right. I had guys who had been in wars and were horribly scarred or amputated, or in wheelchairs or whatever. During pillow talk it would sometimes become obvious that some of them had killed people. Several admitted to me they had erections while they were killing.

MT: It would be better to not call acts of violence sex.

A: You've got to give people an exciting alternative.

MT: An exciting alternative without violence.

A: I'd like to make a great line of pornography that would inspire people to have more loving, satisfying, healthy sex, which would in turn make the world a better place. If no pornography was allowed, I wouldn't get the opportunity to do that. Romantic love, sexual feelings and physical intimacy are the most pleasurable things in many people's lives, next to eating chocolate cake.

MT: We have been trained to believe that sex is the most important thing in life. I don't believe that.

A: I think of our sexualities as a treasure trove of possibilities. To give and receive love, maintain good health, relieve stress . . .

MT: There are other ways to experience fabulous intimacy, beauty and joy. For example, art, friendship, athletics . . .

A: Athletics? Yuk! Church maybe. Singing, chanting, dancing, doing ritual maybe come close. To see a fantastic stripper is an awe-inspiring experience. It is to witness the Divine Feminine. It is prayer. And what often surrounds erotic dancers? Drunk, cigarette-smoking, disrespectful, bad-mannered guys waving measly dollar bills . . .

MT: . . . and waving measly dicks.

A: Pornography, in its purest form, could be a path to enlightenment.

MT: I doubt it. When I hear the word porn, I think of something that is male yuckkiness and lines men's pockets with money . . . and semen. *(We both laugh uproariously.)*

A: Ah, yes, good laughgasm!

MT: Porn is a pocket issue! *(More laughing.)* I haven't laughed so hard in I don't know when.

A: Me too. This was a very intense conversation. I've always dreamed of having this conversation and never even came close. Everyone I've ever met who is anti-porn would never even sit down at the table with me. Except my mother. Oddly enough, I have never really felt that women against porn were my enemies.

MT: I've never had the desire to sit down at the table with a pornographer and have this discussion, but I'm glad to be having it with you. Getting to know you has created trust and that is very precious. By the way, many feminists who are anti-porn don't see the women in it as the enemy either.

A: No, they see us as victims. We don't want to be perceived as victims.

MT: A conversation like this is possible when each of us has freedom of expression and no one is required to change. I don't expect you to become anti-porn, and you don't expect me to become pro-porn.

A: It's been wonderful. Thank you *(big hug)*.

Gabrielle's Midnight Snack with Monika Treut

Monika answered some questions over the Internet about her long acquaintance with Annie.

GABRIELLE CODY: When did you first encounter Annie and what drew you to her work?

MONIKA TREUT: I met Annie by accident when location scouting in San Francisco for my film *Virgin Machine* in 1987. I just bumped into her bosom ballet performance realizing I had heard of Annie before, but I still wasn't prepared for this hilariously funny show. I immediately fell in love with her, we talked afterwards, exchanged phone numbers and then in 1989, I called Annie in New York City and the time was right and we did a short inspired by her *Post-Porn Modernist* show.

GC: Why is Annie Sprinkle a compelling subject to you as a filmmaker?

MT: Part of the attraction probably is that I'm influenced by the very unhumorous way German feminists deal with sex. Annie struck me as someone who combines feminism with wit, fun and plenty of humor. I also have 'used' Annie in my newest film *Gendernauts* as a supporter of Trans people.

GC: Annie is deceptively 'simple.' Her performances are layered with irony and political sophistication.

MT: Yes, in the *Post-Porn Modernist* show, when she shows her cervix and you see the audience lining up to examine it with a flashlight, it makes clear how taboo the inside of the female sex organs are to women and men alike, how unknown, how undiscovered but forbidden, and Annie to me is like a female David Cronenberg who also has crashed the taboo of the inner organs but with male angst, whereas Annie is showing provocative parts with pride and wit.

Movie still of Annie Sprinkle and Alfred Edel in Monika Treut's film *My Father Is Coming*.

GC: Annie often adopts the persona of the 'hooker with the heart of gold.' Is this false naïveté part of the power of her 'female misbehavior,' her ability to turn the so-called 'gaze' back on itself?

MT: Annie is a former prostitute turned artist. And as much as I'm sure pain and frustration are a part of her inventiveness in creating art out of her (not always lovely) experiences as a prostitute, I think Annie tells us to be multiple, to have more choices and more perspectives than just one: just being a prostitute, or just being an artist or just being an academic is probably not enough to be able to float in between different ways of seeing the world.

GC: And anyway, what do you think of the male gaze theory?

MT: I think it's a construction of a handful of frustrated feminists. I'm totally with Camille Paglia on that one. In *Female Misbehavior* she says it's not the male gaze because, honey, I'm using it. I've been using it for too many years, and I'm not on testosterone.

GC: Recently Annie has expressed a lot of ambivalence about her 'hardcore' years. What do you think of her shift toward holistic sexuality and healing, her return to sacred forms of prostitution/sexuality?

MT: I personally believe this is just the natural process of someone maturing, getting older, having new interests in life and being less centered around sex.

Outroduction

Dear Reader. Gee it's been swell.

Possibly you're working on your dissertation, or you saw one of my performances and were curious about the behind-the-scenes aspect of them. Maybe you are a sex worker branching into the art world, or an academic branching into the sex world. You must be interested in theater, and you no doubt are interested in sexuality. Whoever you are, I am grateful for your attention and your interest in my work. I am honored and humbled by it. It is my sincere hope that you got something of use from this book.

It has been a luxury for me to get to communicate with you from an academic, 'non-commercial' perspective. And very flattering to be looked at so studiously by insightful minds. *Hardcore from the Heart* basically picks up where my last book, *Post-Porn Modernist*, left off. With this book I can put yet another decade behind me; it's a great opportunity for closure.

I have been working most pleasurably on this manuscript from the galley of a forty-foot powerboat docked at a small, relatively unpopulated island in paradise. The boat belongs to my loving, sexy girlfriend, Captain Barb, and I now live here with her. It's been a peaceful place to look back on my intense, busy, often controversial career.

This book project has been blessed with some miracles. Just one year ago, when I was on the road performing *Herstory of Porn*, my beautiful Sausalito houseboat home accidentally burned down. I lost most everything I owned: my archives, my photo equipment, wardrobe, computer (and back-up), photographs, etc. Even my two beloved cats, Linda and Tuttles, died in the huge blaze. It was intense! Luckily I had given Gaby Cody most of the material for this book just a few weeks before the fire, or it all would have gone up in smoke.

There was another miracle. News of my fire spread quickly. Friends, peers, and admirers from all over the world insisted on pitching in to help me rebuild. (I never once asked for a thing.) People sent loving letters, presents and extremely generous

Benefit Show, Silent Auction, No Host Bar and D.J. Dancing!

Save the Mermaid
The Annie Sprinkle Fire Show!
Sunday, June 20, 1999
3pm to Midnight ✯ Shows at 4pm & 8pm ✯ Cowell Theatre, Fort Mason

Carol Queen
FetishDiva Midori
Evie Leder
Cosi Fabian
Nina Hartley
M.I. Blue
Fairy Butch
Margo St. James
Michelle Tea
Sini Anderson
Fakir and Cleo Dubois
Jade Blue Eclipse
Kaos Kitty
FatchancebellyDance
Franik Moore and Linda Mac
Dr. Reverend Geoffrey Karen Dior
Juliet "Aunt Peg" Anderson
Some of the Sisters of Perpetual
Indulgence, Inc.
Francesca De Grandis
Molly McGee
Dee Dee Russell
Pat Califia
Ilsa Strix
Rob Brezsny
Joan Jett Black
Kat Sunlove
Dossie Easton
Thoth
Hank Hyena
The Hail Marys
Reverend Shar
David Steinberg
Scarlet Harlot
Pat Califia
Thea Hillman
Candye Kane
Dorrie Lane
Bill Brent
And more!

Carnival Games

Live Auctions

Outdoor Sunset Ritual

Non-Stop Theatre

Isabel Samaras

Tix from City Box Office 415-392-4400 & at Good Vibrations
Info www.houseochicks.com/anniesprinkle.html

**Sponsored by SF Weekly, Climate Theater, Good Vibrations, Lusty Lady,
Queen of Heaven, San Francisco Sex Information, Spectator Magazine & N-ACT**

Poster from the *Save the Mermaid* performance event to benefit Annie Sprinkle after her houseboat fire. Poster produced by Robert Lawrence and Carol Queen, designed by *San Francisco Weekly*, with a drawing by Isabel Samaras.

financial donations. Benefits were organized in Australia, Germany, NYC, LA, Seattle, Austin, etc. San Francisco friends put together a spectacular theater extravaganza with nine hours of performances by 150 fantastic artists and sex workers (a show that is still being talked about today). They raised many thousands of dollars and gave them all to me. Plus when people asked me how they could help, I suggested that they could donate an orgasm (I am a big believer in the power of erotic prayer) and many reportedly did. With all that love coming my way, a big, soft, psychic pillow was created for me to fall back on. The pain of loss was washed away, and my heart burst open. People from the art and theater worlds, the porn, S/M, Tantra, and prostitution worlds were all incredibly generous. To my absolute surprise, I got enormous support from hundreds of people I had never met, but who knew me only through my work. Mostly women. Even some of my old porn fans sent me money anonymously! I had no idea how generous people could be, and how much they cared. I had to learn to receive, big time. The money people gave me not only enabled me to rebuild my life, but to take some time off from having to do paying gigs, to work on this (labor of love) book. This proves my theories, once and for all, that if you make love to the world, the world makes love to you back. And that not all whores, porn stars and avant-garde artists' lives are tragic.

At present I am involved with some wonderful projects. I am in a Ph.D. program at the Institute for the Advanced Study of Human Sexuality. If all goes well, I'll soon be Dr. Sprinkle, sexologist. (All 'big sluts' should eventually get a doctorate.) I am on the board of the glamorous Museum of Sex (see theposition.com) in Manhattan, destined to be an important and unique institution. I am also on the board of the St James Infirmary, the world's first free full-service occupational health care clinic for sex workers in San Francisco. I am a Field Director for the International Sex Worker Foundation for Art, Culture and Education. I continue to perform on stage in theaters internationally, and I do visiting artist presentations at colleges.

As for future projects, I envision two things. One, to buy a large yacht, to create a non-profit floating retreat center for artists and activists to meet, recharge, work and play on the sea. Two, to put together a year-long tour across America made up of a caravan of motor homes filled with performance artists, feminist activists, and sex educators. It would be a 'Women's Sexual Healing Circus,' a sort of national sex-positive 'revival' if you will, so that women in smaller cities and more rural areas can experience the magic and empowerment of creative sexual expression through workshops, shows, actions, private sessions, etc. *MetamorphoSex – The Art of Love* would be part of this tour. (If you would like to be our producer, grant donor, sugar-mama/daddy for either of these projects, we will make it well worth your while.)

These days I fancy myself a mermaid. Mermaids are 'sexsea,' even though they don't wear garter belts and stockings, pose for nude photographs, or go on stage and 'perform' experimental sex acts. They are salty, drenched in seawater, and windblown. They spend their lives combing each others' hair, being joyous and undulating through the water.

Dear Reader, if I can be so bold as to give you some friendly advice: eat your seaweed, try not to censor yourself or others, and be careful with candles. I'd like to climax now with a special blessing, just for you.

Mermaid Fantasea Blessing

May your days be filled with surf and sun,
  Fish and shells and gallons o' fun.

May glittering light rays guide your way.
  In safe harbors may you always stay.

May any troubles simply wash away,
  And may you have many a good hair day.

May you find good friends who will dive in deep.
  On stormy nights have sweet dreams, deep sleep.

May you live a long and healthy life of leisure,
  Filled with pleasure in endless measure.

May you luxuriate in a cozy grotto.
  On full moon night may you win the lotto.

May you have many delicious sensations,
  Get lots o' love and have good vibrations.

Swim with the whales and wear plenty o' pearls,
  Drink tiny bubbles, dance with girls girls girls.

May boundless joy come over you.
  Breach into the clouds and dive anew!

Annie Sprinkle

Selected Performances, Filmography and Bibliography

Live Performances

Burlesque (1980–3) Annie performed her own brand of burlesque called 'Strip Speak' in strip joints across the USA.

Deep Inside Porn Stars (1984) A performance piece created and performed by porn-star support group 'Club 90'. Presented at Franklin Furnace in NYC.

The Prometheus Project (1985) A theater piece by Richard Schechner which featured Annie's *Nurse Sprinkle's Sex Education Class* burlesque show. Presented at the Performing Garage in NYC.

Annie Sprinkle Post-Porn Modernist (1990–5) A one-woman 'play' written and performed by Annie. First directed by Emilio Cubeiro, and later by Willem de Ridder as *Post-Post-Porn Modernist*.

MetamorphoSex (premiered December 1995) A week-long sexuality workshop with twenty-six local women, culminating in three sex-magic performance/rituals which the public was invited to attend.

Hardcore from the Heart (1996–7) A multimedia 'play' written and performed by Sprinkle, featuring Kimberly Silver. Directed by Daniel Banks.

An Intimate, Informal, Show and Tell Evening with Annie Sprinkle (1995 to present) Film clips, sex tips and performance snips. Mostly presented at colleges.

Annie Sprinkle's Herstory of Porn – Reel to Real (1997 to present) Multimedia one-woman show directed by Emilio Cubeiro.

Films and Videos

Deep Inside Annie Sprinkle (1982) A full-length 35mm feature film, written and directed by Annie Sprinkle.

Rites of Passion (1987) A 'tantric erotic adult fairy tale', written and directed by Annie. Produced by Femme Productions.

Linda/Les & Annie: The First Female-to-Male Transsexual Love Story (1990) A 30-minute docudrama, written and co-directed by Annie Sprinkle with Albert Jaccoma and Johnny Armstrong.

My Father Is Coming (1991) A full-length 16mm feature film by Monica Treut.

Female Misbehavior (1992) A 16mm film by Monika Treut with three vignettes, one of which is about Annie, another about Camille Paglia.

The Sluts and Goddesses Video Workshop, or How to Be a Sex Goddess in 101 Easy Steps (1992) A 52-minute video, co-directed, starring and written by Annie. Featuring an all-woman cast.

Annie Sprinkle's Herstory of Porn (1999) A 69-minute feature film, co-directed with Scarlot Harlot. Based on Annie's stage show of the same name. A film diary with clips from many of the sex films she made over twenty-five years. Available from www.goodvibes.com or Erospirit 800-528-1942.

Fire in the Valley (1999) An Intimate Guide to Female Genital Massage, presented with Joseph Kramer. Available from Erospirit 800-528-1942 or www.erospirit.org

Zen Pussy: A Meditation on Eleven Vulvas (1999) Presented with Joseph Kramer. Available from Erospirit 800-528-1942 or www.erospirit.org

HBO's Real Sex (1994 to present; repeatedly re-broadcast) This popular HBO television show has transmitted four segments featuring Annie Sprinkle (more than any other person in the show's history). One segment featured the *Sluts and Goddesses Workshop* (No. 2). Another featured Annie's *Pleasure Activist Playing Cards* (Wild Cards). They also filmed Annie's one-woman shows, *Post-Post-Porn Modernist* (No. 4) and *Herstory of Porn*.

The Art of the Loop (2001) A 16-minute video by Annie Sprinkle, Jeff Fletcher and Scarlot Harlot. A peek at 8-mm sex films from 1954 to 1980.

Workshops and Lectures

Cosmic Orgasm Awareness Week A week-long residential seminar based on the erotic massage rituals of Joseph Kramer. The Body Electric School, Oakland, CA.

Fun with Breath and Energy Orgasms A three-hour ecstasy breathing event.

New Ancient Erotic Massage Rituals and Sensual Magical Mystery Tours Annie is the 'high priestess' for three days of guided group (safe) sex magic rituals utilizing the female genital massage techniques developed with Joseph Kramer.

The Pleasures, Profits and Politics of Female Sexuality A popular lecture at conferences and colleges.

Sacred Sex A three-day, women-only retreat which Annie co-facilitates with Barbara Carrellas, Jwala and sometimes with special guest Linda Montano.

Sacred Sex Technologies: How to Be a Sex Goddess in 101 Easy Steps A one-day course for women.

Sluts and Goddesses A women-only, day-long experimental workshop to explore sexual archetypes.

Annie's official web site is www.heck.com/annie

For an extensive web site about Annie's *Post-Post-Porn Modernist* show see www.bobsart.org

Books by Annie

Annie Sprinkle, Post-Porn Modernist: My Twenty-five Years as a Multimedia Whore 130-page book, with over 400 photographs. Editions published by TORCH Gallery (1991), Art Unlimited (1993), and Cleis Press (1998). PO Box 14684, San Francisco, CA 94114.

Annie Sprinkle's Post-Modern Pin-Ups: Pleasure Activist Playing Cards (1995) Annie's photographs of fifty-six sex-positive women presented as a deck of playing cards. Gates of Heck, New York.

XXXOOO: Love and Kisses from Annie Sprinkle (1997) A two-volume set of mail-art postcards. Gates of Heck, New York.

Books in which Annie Sprinkle appears

Shannon Bell, *Reading, Writing and Rewriting the Prostitute Body*. Indiana University Press, Bloomington and Indianapolis, 1994. Includes a heady chapter on Annie.

Shannon Bell, *Whore Carnival* (1996). Autonomedia, PO Box 568, Williamsburgh Station, Brooklyn, New York, NY 11211-0568. Includes interview with Annie, as well as a story by Shannon about the night she taught Annie about female ejaculation.

Wendy Chapkis, *Live Sex Acts: Women Performing Erotic Labor*. Routledge, New York, 1997. Wendy interviews Sprinkle about her prostitution experiences, and also writes a chapter about her experience in Annie's group erotic massage ritual.

John Heidenry, *What Wild Ecstasy: The Rise and Fall of the Sexual Revolution*. Simon and Schuster, New York, 1997. A fascinating, fact-filled book with several sections about Annie Sprinkle.

Andrea Juno and V. Vale (eds), *Angry Women*. Juno Books, 1992.

Rachel Kaplan and Keith Hennesy (eds), *More Out Than In: Notes on*

Sex, Art, and Community (1995). More Out Than In, c/o 848 Community Space, 848 Divisadero, San Francisco, CA 94117-1506.

Terri Kapsalis, *Public Privates: Performing Gynecology from Both Ends of the Speculum.* Duke University Press, Durham, NC, 1997. Includes a chapter on Sprinkle's 'Public Cervix Announcement.'

Michael Lane and Jim Crotty, *Mad Monks on the Road: A 47,000 Hour Dashboard Adventure.* A Fireside Book, published by Simon and Schuster, New York, 1993. Includes a section about their stay at The Sprinkle Salon in its most outrageous heyday.

Jill Nagle (ed.), *Whores and Other Feminists.* Routledge, London and New York, 1997. Essays on sex work. Annie writes about sex worker burn-out.

Carol Queen, *Real Live Nude Girl: Chronicles of Sex-Positive Culture.* Cleis Press, San Francisco, 1997. Includes a short story about Carol's experience performing the Masturbatorium Ritual on stage with Annie.

Rebecca Schneider, *The Explicit Body in Performance.* Routledge, London and New York, 1997. Excellent history of performance art with an entire chapter devoted to Annie.

Chris Straayer, *Deviant Eyes, Deviant Bodies: Sexual Re-orientation in Film and Video.* Columbia University Press, New York, 1996.

Tristan Taormino and David Aaron Clark (eds), *Ritual Sex* (1997). Rhinocerus Books/Masquerade Books, 801 Second Avenue, New York, NY 10017. Includes a step-by-step recipe for Sprinkle and Joe Kramer's New Ancient Erotic Massage Ritual and Sensual Magical Mystery Tours.

Sheila Marie Thomas, 'Speaking the Unspeakable: Annie Sprinkle's "Prostitute Performances"'. Master's thesis, University of Colorado, 1996.

Linda Williams, *Hard Core: Power, Pleasure and the 'Frenzy of the Visible'.* University of California Press, Berkeley, 1999.

Dirty Looks: Women, Pornography, Power. BFI Publishing, London, 1993. Two academics write about Sprinkle's films and performances.

Voices from the Edge. The Crossing Press, Freedom, CA 95019. Conversations with Jerry Garcia, Ram Das, Annie Sprinkle and others. This is Annie's favorite interview, conducted by David Jay Brown and Rebecca McClean Novick.